praise for *drawing breath*

Inspire means, literally, "to breathe in." *Drawing Breath*, Gayle Brandeis's brilliant new collection of essays, draws inspiration from form—form of the body, form on the page. The result is a compelling, one-of-a-kind pastiche: survey results, a film transcription, the history of a perfume, an exploration into the choral voice, an interview with the self. *Drawing Breath* is both intimate and inventive, deeply personal and culturally relevant. This book, in a word, is breathtaking.

—maggie smith, author of *Goldenrod*

In *Drawing Breath*, Gayle Brandeis writes that she wants her last words to be 'I love you.' In a very real way, this collection of essays is Brandeis' love letter to the world. The writing is powerful yet tender, ferocious yet kind, and always grounded in the body. Brandeis writes with a fierce elegance about her mother's mental illness and suicide, her father's dementia, her own reckoning with body issues, female desire and shame, and a body suffering from long-haul COVID. *Drawing Breath* is a necessary salve to our tumultuous times. When I read the last word of this book, I wanted to turn immediately to the first page and begin again.

—suzanne roberts, author of *Animal Bodies: On Death, Desire, and Other Difficulties*

Every woman has been warned, at some point in her life, to never show certain parts of herself or to share the troubles of her life. We often silence what churns within us and suffer the shaming of our minds, our bodies. Gayle Brandeis writes brilliantly and beautifully about what is hidden. From writing on the cardboard inserts of her father's dry-cleaning shirts at four to writing a memoir in her forties, we follow the map of her (writing) life through states of mental and physical illness; we recognize the mysteries and the powers of the body; we celebrate the unexpected storms of desire in midlife; and we find joy. This biblio-essay collection is a joy! Brandeis lifts up a diverse group of women writers by setting their words alongside her own, creating a chorus of women giving voice to silenced stories. I devoured this book.

—jill talbot, author of *The Way We Weren't: A Memoir*

In *Drawing Breath*, Brandeis reminds us of the strength and fragility of the invisible—our own breath, our hauntings and our haunted, and our relationship with our own art. The brilliance of this collection lies in its vulnerability and willingness to trust the unseen and to guide the reader safely to and through it. This book will remind you of your secret self—the one that has been waiting to be brought back from the shadows into the light--the one that will always see you safely home.

—laraine herring, author of
A Constellation of Ghosts: A Speculative Memoir with Ravens

With *Drawing Breath*, Gayle Brandeis offers her deep attention to pain and loss and grieving and difficulty (as well as love and love and love) in ways that make it all "less scary...more like art than ruin." It is a meditation in essays that can be meaningful and profound for "all humans who want to stay awake and aware." In these pages, we again witness Brandeis's talent for revealing the secrets hidden within the complicated histories of our lives—so that we might more fully inhabit our larger selves by discovering pathways through the painful and tragic.

—brian turner, author of *My Life As A Foreign Country*

drawing breath

drawing

breath

essays on writing, the body, and loss

gayle brandeis

Overcup 🍂 Press

Published in 2023

The following essays were previously published, some under other titles and in slightly different form:

"Portrait of the Writer as a Young Girl" appeared in *Wildness*.
"White Footprints" appeared in *Essay Daily*.
"Drawing Breath" appeared in *The Healing Breath*.
"Spelling" appeared in *Salon*.
"Thunder, Thighs" and "Get Me Away From Here, I'm Dying" appeared in *The Rumpus*.
"We Too" appeared in *Gay Magazine*.
"Her Shadow" appeared in *Ghost Town*.
"Role/Model" and "Self Interview" appeared in *The Nervous Breakdown*.
"Joy" appeared in *The Columbia Journal* and won the Columbia Journal Nonfiction Contest.
"Ghosts in the Ecotone" appeared in *Midnight Breakfast* and was reprinted in *The Kokanee Journal*.
"Arse Poetica" and "Dipping My Mother's Hair in Ink" appeared in *Brevity*.
"Shadow Son" appeared in *The Washington Post* and was a Notable Essay in *Best American Essays, 2019*.
"Anniversary Gifts" appeared in *The New York Times*.
"Press/Pool" appeared in *Jam Tarts*.
"My Parents' Delusions" appeared in *Full Grown People*.
"Eating the Food of the Dead appeared in *The Normal School* and was a Notable Essay in *Best American Essays, 2020*.
"Figure Skating" appeared in *Pangyrus*.
"Rib/Cage" appeared in *DIAGRAM*.
"Going to Seed" appeared in The Nevada Humanities *Heart to Heart* series.

Cover Art: Travis "Bedelgeuse" Bedel
Cover Design: Sean Paul Levine
Book Design: Jenny Kimura

ISBN: 979-8-9856527-1-0

Library of Congress Control Number: Available upon request.

Printed in Canada

Overcup Press
4207 SE Woodstock Blvd. #253
Portland, OR 97206
Overcupbooks.com

gaylebrandeis.com

My body experiences, deep down inside,
one of its panicky cosmic adventures.
I have volcanoes on my lands.
But no lava: what wants to flow is breath.
And not just any old way.
The breath "wants" a form.
"Write me!"

—Hélène Cixous, from *Coming to Writing*

previous works by
gayle brandeis

Many Restless Concerns
The Art of Misdiagnosis
The Selfless Bliss of the Body
Delta Girls
Self Storage
The Book of Dead Birds
Fruitflesh

contents

introduction

I WAS A COLLECTOR AS A KID—COINS, PUFFY STICKERS, scented dinosaur-shaped erasers, glass animals, Nancy Drew books, Breyer horses, and the like—and took special care to arrange my treasures just so, even though I was (still am) a girl prone to mess. I loved them all, but my favorite collections by far were the shells and rocks and sea glass I'd gather on the shore of Lake Michigan across the street from my apartment. Gifts the beach would offer up as my feet sank into wet sand, eyes trained for glint and whorl. Gifts that begged to come home with me, gifts that felt just right in my hand, gifts I loved to splash with water and watch their hidden pinks and greens flare, then fade, gifts I'd arrange and rearrange inside my many-compartmented jewelry box to see how they looked next to each other, to see what they might say to one another, mica winking at a pebble of frosty blue glass, a geode sharing its jagged sparkle with the inner blush of a freshwater snail shell.

Organizing this essay collection felt akin to arranging these rocks and shells, finding resonances and conversation between them, casting off ones that no longer sparked my heart. I didn't write these essays with a collection in mind—each one came to me as its own stone, shaped by the tides and grit of my life—but ongoing threads of curiosity and grief and devotion course through them like veins of shared minerals, placing them on the same map, a map made of something warmer than stone. A map of body and word and the breath that animates and unites them.

A map of my writing life.

While most of the essays in this collection are far more recent, the title essay, "Drawing Breath," is more than twenty years old, originally written as a critical paper when I was working toward my MFA in Fiction at Antioch University, mentored by the brilliant, visionary Alma Luz Villanueva. I'd been fascinated by the connection between writing and the body for many years by that point; I've been a writer and dancer since I was very young and created my own BA concentration at the University of Redlands' Johnston Center for Integrative Studies—Poetry and Movement: Arts of Expression, Meditation, and Healing—to explore my beloved arts more deeply, graduating with that degree in 1990. I often said I wanted to dance in a way that was as articulate as language, to write in a way that was as muscular as dance, and I found the nexus of those two arts was the body, the breath. I divided my critical paper into inhales and exhales to meld form and content, exploring my own lived experience of breath with each inhale, then looking outward with each exhale, delving into research related to breath and writing. In some ways, this created the template for my life as a creative nonfiction writer—all my essays since have tended to look both inward toward embodiment and outward toward the world (and many have played with structure, as well). Organizing this collection around different types of breath is an extension of this template, a reminder that our breath (and our writing!) can take so many forms.

The first section of the collection, "Eupnea: Quiet Breathing," holds essays grounded in childhood and a burgeoning relationship with language. It includes another vintage essay, "Spelling," published by *Salon* in 1999—my first major byline—about my then–five-year-old daughter learning to write, an essay that remains one of my favorites, even after all these years, an essay that gave me the chance to celebrate just how magical the process of writing can be.

The next section, "Hyperaeration: Increased Lung Volume," looks at ways women (cis/trans/nonbinary) can support and empower one another, ways we can increase one another's volume on and off the page, individually and in chorus. I share several women-identifying voices along with my own in these essays—those who write in the first-person plural, those who responded to my questionnaire about thighs, those who helped me after sexual assault, those whose writing about their mothers speaks to and for my own complicated maternal relationship.

The essays in "Ponopnea: Painful Breathing" investigate my mother's suicide and are the most grueling essays I've written. If you've read my memoir, *The Art of Misdiagnosis*, some of the passages will likely sound familiar. I wrote these essays before I was ready to write the book; they helped gird me for the longer project, and I grafted some cuttings from them into my memoir as it evolved. "Get Me Away From Here, I'm Dying," which appeared in *The Rumpus* in 2012, was an especially significant essay for me: it was the first piece I'd published about my mother's suicide, and the day it came out, I felt so vulnerable and exposed, I thought I might pass out or throw up. The generous response the piece received encouraged me to commit to writing my memoir.

"Tachypnea: Increased Breathing Rate" examines the process of writing and publishing *The Art of Misdiagnosis,* a process that was both profoundly difficult and profoundly transformative. I hope this section will be of special interest to those writing a memoir, or considering writing one, as well as those curious about the process and experience of laying one's life bare on the page.

The key word in the next section's title, "Orthopnea: Breathlessness in Lying Down Position Relieved by Sitting Up or Standing" is "relieved"; the essays here unpack some of the gifts that have risen from painful experience, such as the gift of my friendship with the man who had been convinced I was his biological mother in my viral *Washington Post* essay, "Shadow Son"; the gift of reconciling with my husband after I blew up our marriage; the gift of reigniting my activism in the Trump era (as much as I wish it hadn't been necessary). The essay "Anniversary Gifts" in this section is a mash-up of two essays published by *The New York Times:* "Our Anniversaries Matched Their Gifts," which appeared in the Ties section, and "We Wanted to Split Up. OK Cupid Had Other Ideas," which appeared in Modern Love.

Rounding out the book are the sections "Bradypnea: Decreased Breathing Rate," whose essays chronicle my beloved father's decline and death, and "Apnea: Absence of Breath," whose essays take on our pandemic era, including how my dance with presumed long COVID has affected my body, mind, and writing voice. I confront my own mortality in this section, but it's fair to say this entire collection is charged with the presence of our mortality, charged with awareness that the breath in our dear bodies will someday cease, our inhales and exhales framed by endless silence.

As someone with asthma and other respiratory issues, breath has always been somewhat fraught for me, and breath, of course, has become a culturally fraught subject during the time of coronavirus—

Breath as danger: with an airborne virus like COVID, we can literally kill one another with an exhale.

Breath as injustice: George Floyd told Derek Chauvin and his fellow officers, "I can't breathe" more than twenty times before Chauvin's knee took his breath forever.

Breath as appropriation and division: "I can't breathe"—a phrase heard and seen often at 2020 protests after Floyd's death, a phrase used in protests since Eric Garner's 2014 videotaped chokehold death, a phrase uttered by Elijah McClain and Manuel Ellis and other Black men lost to racialized police violence—was co-opted by white, anti-mask protestors who equated mask mandates with Nazi Germany, people who wanted their breath unfettered, no matter the cost to the most vulnerable around them.

These anti-mask protestors will likely never have their own breath cut short by police officers, and I share that privilege, even as I don't share their position. I touch upon my whiteness in some of these essays and know continuing to investigate this privilege, and how my Jewishness intersects with and complicates it, will be a lifelong endeavor. So will continuing to listen to BIPOC writers and speakers and friends who illuminate unjust systems, reminding me we may all breathe the same atmosphere, but not everyone has the same access to clean air. Their voices help me recognize my complicity within these systems and point me toward doing better.

The word "essay" shares the same root as "assay," a verb used in metallurgy, chemistry, alchemy, meaning to test or weigh a substance to determine its composition. I think back again to my childhood collections, my intuitive groupings of pebble and shell, my attempts to determine which rocks were formed from cooled magma, which rocks were formed from the skeletons of beings who came before, which rocks were formed from the fusing of other rocks via heat and pressure. I similarly tested and weighed these essays as I put this collection together, tracing their origins of heat and grief and heart. These essays tested me as I wrote and revised and ordered them, too, showing me what I'm made of (for better and for worse), their weight aching within me until I was ready to release them from my body, breathe them out into the air.

Thank you—from the bottom of my heart and lungs and all the rest of me—for breathing them in.

I

EUPNEA:
quiet breathing

portrait of the writer as a young girl

THE GIRL WRITES HER FIRST POEM WHEN SHE IS four years old:

> Blow, little wind,
> Blow the trees, little wind,
> Blow the seas, little wind,
> Blow me until I am free, little wind.

Somehow, even at this young age, the girl knows writing can be a wind that blows through her, makes her more spacious inside, freer. She feels it from the very start. She'll still feel it decades later.

The girl's favorite writing surface is the cardboard tucked into her dad's dress shirts when they come back from the dry cleaners. Some of the folded, cling-wrapped button-downs are stacked inside the bone-colored armoire in her parents' room; others are stacked in the top shelf of the closet, where her winter coats hang over her rubber boots. She slices the wrappers open with her finger and slides the pieces of cardboard out, the shirts slumping inside the plastic like a sigh.

One side of the cardboard is slick and white and smells a little bit sour, like paste; the other side is brown and rough, nubby like oatmeal, and smells more like sawdust. She lies on her stomach on the living room rug and lists titles of stories she wants to write. Her crayon scuds across the white side, leaving waxy shreds in its wake; on the rough side, the crayon leaves a deeper, thicker tread. She feels her breath push into the carpet as her words push their way onto the stiff page, the ghosts of her father's shirtsleeves wrapped around it like a hug.

The girl is shy—she makes her sister order for her at Arby's, rarely ever raises her hand in class—but when she writes, she's brave. She creates a neighborhood newspaper and interviews neighbors and sells subscriptions door-to-door. Writing is her superpower, the caped heart that flies inside her mild-mannered skin.

The girl sees her mom write "poison pen" letters when she is upset about something. She watches the letter-writing campaigns her mom spearheads change things: a traffic light installed at a dangerous intersection near her school; guns and ammunition removed from her local Kmart after some violence. The girl starts to write her own letters—letters to the editor railing at the teenage boys who throw rocks at ducks at the beach, at people who throw trash out the windows of their cars. She writes to President Carter to ask how she can stop pollution and receives a "Keep America Clean" pack in return. She takes the bright orange garbage bags, printed with Woodsy Owl—"Give a Hoot, Don't Pollute"—to the beach and picks up pop-top tabs and stray wrappers, knowing she has a presidential order to do so. She sends a letter in solidarity to Amy Carter after the first daughter gets in trouble for reading at a state dinner, and Amy Carter writes back. The girl tacks the letter, along with a photo of Amy Carter torn from a magazine, over her bed.

The girl's mom's Uncle Jimmy, who looks like W.C. Fields and lives in a men's hotel in Cleveland and pulls silver dollars from her ears, tells her mom he is looking for someone to write his life story.

The girl immediately offers, sure she can tackle the biography of a 76-year-old man who was raised in an orphanage and fed her mom bear meat when her mom was a girl. Jimmy writes back to let her mom know a child could never write his story; he wants his book to focus on women who performed unusual sexual acts. The girl has little understanding of what usual sexual acts even entail, but she is intrigued. She wonders if this is what people write about when they're grown.

When the girl touches herself, she swirls words into the place between her legs, whatever words spring to mind—peanut, bird, Zamboni. She doesn't know this is about sex—these feelings are just a sweet gift from her body. Words and pleasure become inter-twined, become the same thing. She's introduced to shame when her mom catches her and tells her she's too old to be doing such a thing; body and mind start to split then, body and word. It will be quite a while before they're reunited. She'll later wonder what a transcript of all those words she ground into herself would say if she could somehow unspool it from her body, that list of words written on her most tender skin.

The girl likes to write about what is hidden—her series, "The Elves and I," follows creatures who live in the drainpipe in front of her building; her first "novel," *The Secret World*, is a twenty-page, thinly veiled knockoff of her favorite book, *The Secret Garden*. Her teacher has it laminated and spiral-bound and put in the school library; it gets its own card in the card catalog, her name in the same wooden drawer as Judy Blume's. Her first taste of being a published author.

The girl fills a plaid-covered "Anything Book" with short sto-ries. In "School Daze," a teacher has plastic surgery and turns psychotic. In "Never Say Diet," an anorexic woman makes her whole family eat a diet of grapefruit and rice before she's rushed to the hospital. In "Rocky," a girl tries to cope with going blind, aided by her trusty horse. The girl doesn't know she will write about these same themes—mental and physical illness and the mysteries of the body—the rest of her life.

The girl stands at her bedroom window in her pink baby-doll nightgown, a wisp of cotton candy nylon. The Humpty Dumpty lamp on her dresser is on; she knows people can see into her fifth-floor window if they choose to glance up, can see this ten-year-old girl who feels both younger inside and, somehow, much, much older.

The building next to hers looks like a castle from the front—red brick, turrets, a sunken garden courtyard that she likes to sneak into—but from the side, it looks unfinished, a paler brick, exposed beams, stark concrete steps.

The girl touches the yellow-and-white gingham drape that hangs by her side, the one that matches her bedspread, her puffy rocking chair, the yellow and white, faux-bamboo bedroom set. She knows she must glow in this window. She might even look sexy, whatever that means.

The girl wants to understand the backs of things, the unfinished sides of things, the place where the castle ends and real life begins. She shifts her head so she can see Lake Michigan undulating across the street in the dusk, a pewter gray mirror. She wants someone to look up and see her. She wants to be seen, not just the front of her—the frothy pink, the princess—but behind that: the inside of her notebook, her soaring caped heart, the parts she's been warned to never show.

white footprints

I AM LEARNING THE NAMES OF MY CHILDHOOD WORLD.
I learn the weed I loved—the one with smooth, green leaves circled around a tall spike, a spike I used to love to run my fingers down, strip it of its little green buds—is called plantain. Like the fruit but not like the fruit. I learn plantain is a healing plant—if you chew or crush it and press it to your skin, it can stop bleeding, neutralize bugbites, bring splinters to the surface. I had thought it was a Midwestern plant; when I saw it for the first time in California, years after I had left Illinois, I fell to my knees, fell back into my child body. (I learn it's also called "white man's footprint," learn it was brought to America by colonizers, learn my journey West mimicked its own. So many white footprints.)

I learn the boulders that line the shore of Lake Michigan, boulders I spent hours scrambling over, smelling their cool mineral breath, their texture embedding itself into my palms and knees, are called riprap, are there to slow erosion. Riprap feels like too silly a name, too close to riffraff, to the trip trap of goats on an ogre's bridge. These stones are majestic, the vertebrae of a giant serpent hugging the edge of the lake. The backbone of my life.

I knew the name Potawatomi. Now I learn Odawa, now I learn Ho-Chunk, Menominee, Sac and Fox. Now I learn the names of peoples ripped from the land so I could one day call it home.

I learn the name Chicago comes from the Algonquin *shikaakwa*, meaning striped skunk and onion, meaning pungence.

I learn the shores of Chicago once reeked with wild onions and leeks and ramps. I never found members of the allium family as a child but can picture myself pulling them from the sand, can picture myself biting into those sulfurous bulbs.

There's so much beneath the surface.

So much that burns in the throat.

drawing breath

i n h a l e

I blow a circle of breath onto the
back seat window of our Chevy
Impala, then write on the
slippery surface with my ten-
year-old finger. As the dark
world whizzes by, light
from a row of street lamps
seeps through my words,
turning them luminous,
turning the condensed
beads of my breath into
stars. Dazzled, I smear
them with my palm, then
blow a new puff of air so I
can write more. My right hand
is wet from all the moisture in
my lungs, all the words that have
shaped themselves there. In the
morning, if the sun hits the window
just right, I can see some of those words
glint on the glass, ghosts of my drawn
breath.

∽

I watch my son and daughter
play with a set of Blow Pens. The
bright words on the box identify it
as an "air coloring system." The air
my kids color is their own. They put the
mouthpiece end of a pen between their
lips, then blow. A fine mist of color sprays the
paper. The kids form words, draw butterflies, fill
in stencils, with subtle movements of their mouths
and hands. They are literally drawing breath, their breath
mapped out on the page in every shade of the rainbow.
I watch them blow and color, blow and write their names, and I
think, this is what writing is…finding a way to let our breath live
on the page. Finding a way to tint each exhale so the colors that
live inside us can find their way out into the world. Dragging our
fingers through the vapor of our lungs and seeing what shapes
we leave behind.

∽

Seven centuries ago, Rumi said, "Here's the new
rule: break the wineglass,/and fall toward the
glassblower's breath." Here's the new rule I
propose now: break open a poem, a sentence, a paragraph, a word, and fall
toward the breath of the writer. Just
like glass, our words are shaped
by breath and fire. Breath is an
integral part of our language,
intimately woven into our

alphabet, our grammar, our creative process. I'll attempt to
break open the goblet of writing here and seek out the
breath that swirls inside, the breath we as writers
sometimes catch, sometimes free. The breath we
draw, the breath we draw from, whenever we
sit down to write.

In "Poem Out of Childhood," Muriel
Rukeyser instructs, "Breathe-in experience, breathe-out poetry." The
pulse of our lungs mirrors the rec-
iprocity between self and world
that exists within the act of
writing. "There is a furnace
in our cells," writes Diane
Ackerman, "and when we
breathe, we pass the world
through our bodies, brew
it lightly, and turn it loose
again, gently altered for
having known us."

e x h a l e

In most cultures, the word "breath"
is synonymous with life force, or spirit.
Spiritus in Latin, pneuma in Greek,
ruach in Hebrew, prana in Sanskrit, chi
in Chinese, nilch'i in Navajo, all link breath
with vitality, breath with the divine, creative
spark. John Fire Lame Deer, a Lakota elder, calls
upon "Woniya wakan—the holy air—which renews all
by its breath. Woniya, Woniya wakan—spirit, life, breath,

renewal—it means all that."
In the Judeo-Christian Genesis
story, "the Lord God formed
man *of*/the dust of the ground,
and breathed/into his nostrils the
breath of life;/and man became a
living soul." The Taoist treatise *Huai-nan*
Tzu instructs that everything originally
came from one "Primordial Breath," which
split into "the light ethereal Yang breath, which
formed Heaven; and the heavier, cruder Yin breath,
which formed Earth."
We are made of breath; breath enlivens us, acts as conduit
between ourselves and the elements, ourselves and whatever
we might consider the divine.
It's not surprising that breath has long been connected to creative
human expression, to Word. The Navajo believe "it is only by
means of Wind that we talk. It exists at the tip of our tongues,"
which in turn is similar to these words from Ogotemmêli, a Dogon
diviner in Mali: "The life force which is the Bearer of the Word,
which *is* the Word, leaves the mouth in the form of breath,
or water vapour, which is water and which is Word."
In *Eros the Bittersweet*, Anne Carson writes: "For
the ancient Greeks, breath is perception, breath
is emotion. The phrenes seem to be roughly
identifiable with the lungs in ancient physiological theory and to contain the spirit
of breath as it comes and goes....
Words are 'winged' in Homer when
they issue from the speaker and
'unwinged' when they are kept
in the phrenes unspoken."
Our lungs are wings inside

our chest, beating with each word we speak, letting us soar
to dizzying heights. David Abram, author of *The Spell of
the Sensuous: Perception and Language in a More-than-
Human World*, writes: "In the absence of writing,
human utterance, whether embodied in songs,
stories, or spontaneous sounds, was inseparable from the exhaled breath." He goes
on to say breath *did* hold a place in
early forms of writing, especially
within the traditional Hebrew
aleph-bet. Vowels weren't
written down, he theorized,
because as sounded breath,
they are akin to ruach, the
breath of the divine, and to
write them down would
be to attempt to make
the invisible visible. The
absence of written vowels
allowed both the divine and
the natural world to breathe
through the page.
In the eighth century BCE,
Greek scribes adapted the
Hebrew aleph-bet for their own
use, and, in the process, added written
vowels to their symbology. This, according to Abram, had dire consequences. The
absence of vowels had "provided the pores,
the openings in the linguistic membrane through
which the invisible wind—the living breath—could
still flow between the human and the more-than-human
worlds." Once these written vowels entered human

consciousness, the individual self became, for the first
time, sealed inside the skull,
cut off from the rich swirl of
life. Words were suddenly severed
from the landscape, from the senses;
abstractions began to multiply in a
rarified, unbreathable air—not the air
warmed by the lungs— the air that teems
with scent and song. Fortunately, writers have
always found a way to punch through this new
membrane, to let breath seep back into the language,
to let our shifting selves seep back into the world, back
into the Word.

i n h a l e

I open my throat and let vowels pour out. The letter "A" buzzes
from mouths all around me, filling the room with rich, multilayered
vibration. I can feel the vowel burrow its hum down into my
belly. A collective breath is taken, then "E" begins to suf-
fuse the air. I can imagine Rilke guiding us, saying,

feel how your breath is still increasing
space.
Among the beams of the dark bel-
fries let
yourself ring out...

I am a member of Theater of
Life, an experimental theater troupe grounded in

meditation practice. We begin each rehearsal in silence, following our breath, until the director, Denise Taylor, asks
us to chant vowels, extending each one the length of a
full exhale. All of the vowels—a, e, i, o, u—have a
different frequency, a different vibration in the
throat. Each one fills my breath, rocks my
whole body. I am amazed by the power
of these vowels, how they expand to
enter every bit of space in the room,
how they saturate the breath with
their pure, open sound.
I think about how I use these
vowels countless times every
day—when I speak, when
I write—but I have never
understood their full
power, their full breath-
taking, breath-shaking
glory until now. With each
new letter, I can feel the
walls I've constructed within
my lungs, around my "self,"
begin to break down. I can
feel my self and the world flow
together, a free and vital exchange.

e x h a l e

Inspiration is inseparable from the breath—its
root, inspirare, literally means "to breathe in."
Jane Hirshfield writes: "All written work retains some
trace, however faint, of this initial sanctity of the Word: The

breath inhabiting Logos and
the breath of inspiration are
the same, each bringing new
life into the empty places of
earth."
Sometimes the call to write is felt
in the breath first—a gasp, a catch in
the chest. The breath fills us, and asks, in
turn, to be filled with language as we breathe
back out.
"Inspiration is unobstructed breath, with that feeling of a hollow body, like the body as a reed," Allen
Ginsberg said in an interview, "a kind of straight spine in
a state of complete alertness and awakeness and the air passing
in and out of the column—the body becoming a column of air."
Breath is such a powerful metaphor for, and fount of, creativity,
because it exists right at the nexus of body and mind. It is our
only physiological function that is at once voluntary and involun-
tary, shifting between the two modes like an alternating current,
dipping equally into both conscious and unconscious awareness.
The breath can take us deep into our bodies, as well as
up into abstract realms of thought, reminding us how
interconnected, how inseparable these two paths
truly are. As Gretel Ehrlich writes, "This whole
business of dividing body and mind is ludi-
crous. After all, the breath that starts the
song of a poem, or the symphony of a
novel—the same breath that lifts me
into the saddle—starts in the body,
and at the same time, enlivens the
mind."

i n h a l e

My worst. Asthma. Attack. Ever.
I. Am. Six. Teen.
My mother. Drives me. To the emer. Gen.
Cy. Room.
I hear her. Murmur. Oh no oh no oh
no. As she watches. Me gasp. For.
Breath.
In the E.R. I breathe. Into. A.
Spirometer. It. Measures. The.
Flow. Of. My. Breath. It.
Bare. Ly. Moves. I. Think.
Of. Spirographs. I played
with. As a child. How
sometimes. The little
wheel. Inside the other.
Wheel. Would slip. And
the pencil. Would. Make.
A lopsided. Circle. An awkward. Skip. Of the graphite. A
mess. On the page. And this. Is
how. My breath feels. In my lungs.
Later I am admitted into my own
hospital room, a mask across my nose
and mouth channeling misty broncodi-
lators into my lungs, adrenaline pumping
into my body through an I.V. When night
falls, I can't sleep. I write poems all night long.
One after the other. I can't stop them. Maybe it's
the adrenaline turning me manic, churning frantic
words out of my veins. Or maybe I'm just so happy to be

able to breathe, so happy to
have life flow unobstructed
through my body again—in/
out, in/out—that the words flow
with this joy.

e x h a l e

Breath enters our writing in many guises. It
especially loves to cloak itself in poetry. The same
word means both "to breathe" and "to make a poem"
in at least one Inuit dialect. Poet Edward Hirsch reminds
us, "For most of human history, poetry has been an oral art.
It retains vestiges of that orality always. Writing is not speech. It is
graphic inscription, it is visual emblem. Nonetheless: 'I made it out
of a mouthful of air,' W.B. Yeats boasted in an early poem. As, indeed,
he did. As every poet does."
Breath turns visible by inscribing its rhythms into our poems. As
Allen Ginsberg says, "Nobody's got any objection to even iambic
pentameter if it comes from a source deeper than the mind—
that is to say, if it comes from the breathing and the belly
and the lungs."
And the breath has as much influence on the
prose sentence as it does on the poetic line, as
Ben Jonson notes in *The English Grammar.*

There resteth one generall Affection
of the whole, dispersed thorow every
member thereof, as the bloud is
thorow the body; and consisteth
in the Breathing, when we pro-
nounce any Sentence; For,

whereas our breath is by nature so short, that we cannot con-
tinue without a stay to speake long together; it was thought
necessarie, as well as for the speakers ease, as for the
plainer deliverance of things spoken, to invent this
meanes, whereby men pausing a pretty while,
the whole speech might never the worse be
understood.

i n h a l e

The Dr. Seuss book crackles
and sighs as my dad opens
the cover and flips to the
first page. I snuggle down
under my own covers
and wait for the story
to start. "Fox" is the
first word, and it gusts
out, scented with Colgate
toothpaste, between the
small gap in my dad's front
teeth. I breathe in the sound,
the word, the story, breathe in my
dad reading it to me. The book is
full of rhymes, full of tongue twisters,
and I can feel Dr. Seuss slowly leading
us both into hysteria, tumbling one wild
word after another into my dad's mouth, into
my ear—an unpunctuated rush of puddles and
paddles and poodles and noodles—until we both
collapse, laughing, breathless—against the headboard.
After my dad leaves a minty good night kiss on my cheek, I

pick up the book and read it
to myself, Dr. Seuss's words
twisting my tongue, tickling
my lungs, making me gasp for
air all over again as I wait for a
comma, a period, to save me.

e x h a l e

The relationship between reader and writer is a
deeply intimate one, reciprocal as breath, as essayist
Sven Birkerts explores: "Ree-durr—Rye-turr, Ree-durr—
Rye-turr...passing along the very spirit breath itself, the long,
pneumatic hiss on which all meaning rides.... Ree-durr—Rye-
turr....The eerie, necessary interchange—a surge of animated air
as the one breathes in and the other breathes out."
Each semicolon, each period on the page tells the reader when and
how to breathe. As British essayist Pico Iyer writes, "The Gods,
they say, give breath and they take it away. But the same could be
said—could it not?—of the humble comma."
When we, as writers, are aware of the breath-wielding
power of punctuation, we have more knowledge
about how we can touch our readers' breath.
Charles D'Ambrosio notes: "It's very intimate,
and there's an enormous responsibility. With
long sentences, you're pushing someone,
you're taxing them; you're asking them
to give over their rhythm for your
rhythm, their breathing for your
breathing. You have to know that
you have the potential to get
that close."

i n h a l e

The ultrasound technician squeezes clear goo
onto my belly, then presses the rubber paddle
down against my solar plexus. I watch
the inside of my body swirl and pulse
in grainy black-and-white on the
screen. It looks like outer space,
full of gauzy constellations, but
it's not. It's inner space. My
own undulating galaxy. I look
for the planet of my spleen,
the organ that may be
enlarged, the reason for
this ultrasound, but I
can't discern it in all this
stardust throb.
"Hold your breath," the
technician tells me. I inhale,
let the breath expand my ribs.
She pushes a few buttons on
the machine, presses the rubber
paddle deeper into my skin. "You
can breathe," she says, easing the
paddle up.
I let the air rush back out of my lungs,
then ask, "Do I have to hold my breath so
everything will stay still?"
"That's part of it." She inserts a new film below
the screen. "But it also expands your organs,
lengthens them, makes them easier to see."
She turns me onto my side.

"Hold your breath," she says
again, then points to the monitor. "Here," she says. "This is
your gallbladder. See how it flattens out when you inhale?"
I watch a black hole on the
screen stretch into a river. I am
amazed by how my whole body
responds to breath, how every organ is
affected by the rhythm of my lungs. What
stories lie inside all these comets, these nebu-
lae? How do the stories change with each breath
I take, each breath I hold?

e x h a l e

When we are in the thick of the creative flow, we often hold our
breath. This is different from chronic breath holding that blocks the
breath, inhibits it, resists fully embodied experience. "To breathe
little is to feel little," writes Alexander Lowen in *The Betrayal of
the Body*. The kind of breath holding we experience while
writing marks an opening into rather than a closing
off—it signals an entrance into the altered creative
state, an entrance into awe. Our writing often
takes our breath away from the very moment
of inspiration. "[Writing] captured me...,"
writes Hélène Cixous. "From some
bodily region. I don't know where.
'Writing' seized me, gripped me,
around the diaphragm, between
the stomach and the chest, a
blast dilated my lungs and I
stopped breathing."

When our writing takes our breath away, we enter a vibrant,
fertile pause. In her poem "Why I Dance," Peggy Gwi-
Seok Hong writes, "After the exhale and before
the inhale is where/the answer lies. I wait here
and listen." We often inhabit this pause as
we write. We pull our breath in, suspend
it, and dive deep into ourselves for an
answer before we breathe out again.

i n h a l e

I close the door behind me in
the sensory-deprivation tank
and lower myself into the
shallow salt water, warm
as blood. I lean back,
and my hair fans behind
me like a mermaid's; the
saline holds my naked body
in its buoyant embrace. I am
weightless, suspended in darkness. My eyes disappear into
the absence of light, but my other
senses are not deprived. I smell salt,
can taste it against my palate. My skin
is alive, caressed by the gentle rocking of
the water. My ears receive each throb of
my heart, each inhale and exhale of lung. The
whole tank soon becomes a chamber of breath. I
feel myself riding my breath, my body rising and falling like waves. At some point, my edges seem to dissolve,
and I become all breath. No skin, no bones, no "me"—all

that is left is rhythm, the
whole world expanding and
contracting in sweet, soft
shushes. "The universe," poet
Gary Snyder reminds us, "...is a
vast breathing body." It's a feeling I
recognize—the same selfless, rhythmic
spaciousness I sometimes enter when a
poem decides to breathe itself through me.

e x h a l e

To open ourselves to the winds of inspiration, we have let the
ego, the vowel "I," seep out of its brittle, written shell.
Our breath reminds us we are connected to the landscape, the
atmosphere, connected to one another. It reminds us that even
though we each have our own, unique voice, even though we each
have rich inner lives, we are not separate from one another, or from
the world that surrounds us. Each day, we breathe in millions of
air molecules that have passed through endless lungs and
leaves. We add ourselves to this splendid mix when we
breathe back out, all of us part of the same pulsing,
breathing tide. No one's breath is more important than anyone else's. We are all bonded by
the invisible, life-giving wind. Our voices
swirl in chorus on its currents.
In her poem "Fire," Joy Harjo writes:

a woman can't survive
by her own breath
alone

...

look at me
i am not a separate woman
i am a continuance
of blue sky
i am the throat
of the sandia mountains
a night wind woman
who burns
with every breath
she takes.

inhale

Every night before I
go to sleep, I listen to
my son and daughter
breathe. Their breath is
my lullaby—I can't fall
asleep without hearing it. I
am inestimably soothed by
the couplets of their lungs.
I remember when they were
babies, sometimes I couldn't tell
whether or not they were breathing. I would put the flat of my palm
against their small backs until I could
feel the subtle rise and fall. My touch
often woke them, their squall of shock sweet
to my ears. I was always so happy to know their
lungs were full of good, fierce breath.
Now they breathe loudly as they sleep—they honk
and snort, and sometimes sigh. I follow each throaty sound

with great pleasure, breathe
it deeply into my own lungs.
I think of the ancient Keres
blessing, translated by Paula
Gunn Allen:

I add my breath to your breath
That our days may be long on the Earth
That the days of our people may be long
That we may be one person

The breath connects, blesses all of us. It is my favorite
song in the world, this breath, this song we all sing—Inhale:
I am. Exhale: *alive.* It is the only song we really know, the only
song we really write, the song our bodies keep belting out into the
darkness, over and over, again and again: *I am. Alive. I am. Alive.
We are. Alive. We are. Alive.*

e x h a l e

Our living breath is made all the more precious by our
awareness of our own mortality. Breath frames our
time on this earth—we take in our first breath
right after we are born, we give out our last
breath right before we die. In between
these two breaths, our lives are governed
by the dance of inhale and exhale, a
rhythm that we know will one day
expire, literally breathe itself out
and away. Poet Robert Hass
reports:

*I was doing a radio call-in show up on the Oregon Coast, and
all sorts of people called in to recite poems they'd written at
one time or another in their lives. One old man called
in with a poem that he entitled "Thinking About
Cole Porter on Wake Island"—the only poem
he'd written in his life he wrote when he was
a Marine in the Second World War. And
this prompted a guy from the local state
prison to call and say: "I'll tell you
what poetry is. If you say anything
and know it's your breath and
that you have this one life and
this is the only time this breath
is ever going to pass through
your body in just this way, I
don't care if it's a laundry
list you read, it's poetry."
And I thought, that's
pretty good: poetry is mortal
breath that knows it's mortal.*

This breath that fills our
bodies, this breath that fills
our alphabet, our grammar,
our creative process, this breath
that connects us, operates against a
backdrop of its own silence. Silence that
rises in the pause between each inhale and
exhale, silence that hums itself out toward
infinity. Silence that will one day claim us as
its own. It's no wonder we wish to turn our living
breath into luminous swirls of language; it's no wonder
we wish to color our breath, draw it on the page, while we

still have breath to draw.
"Against the silence," Bob
Shacochis writes, "we move,
we create. We breathe. Exhale."

spelling

WHEN JEWISH CHILDREN BEGIN TO STUDY TORAH, rabbis will sometimes give them a spoonful of honey so they'll always associate learning with sweetness. I brought home alphabet cookies with a similar intention, figuring they'd provide a delicious reading lesson for my five-year-old daughter. I could picture us at the table together, spelling CAT and LOVE and APPLE on our plates, mouths full of shortbread and sugar and the lingering sweetness of words.

When I got home, I discovered Hannah had been sent to her room for some minor infraction, and she was not happy about it. Had she whined? Maybe. Had she cried? Most likely. I wasn't there to hear her protests. But she had found a way to document her experience. She had *written*.

I should mention Hannah had never written anything on her own before this, other than her name and the names of our family members. She had never constructed a sentence, had never sat down with the intention of getting her thoughts on paper, but somehow, in the hour I was gone, she pretty much figured out the whole writing process.

As I walked through her door, Hannah handed me a piece of paper.

"DYR MOM," it said. "DED IS ALWYS MEYN."

Rough drafts of the letter were scattered around her room: "DRY MOM," one began. "DYR MAM," read another.

I was blown away. Not only had Hannah written a sentence for the first time—she had edited her own work! It took me years to make friends with the revision process; Hannah shook hands with it right from the start. My heart filled to bursting—my little girl, a writer!

My husband was amazed, too, although he was not completely thrilled to be the villain of her first literary undertaking. This gave us a peek into what it must feel like to read a daughter's memoir. Wait, the author's parents must want to say, that's not the whole story! We bought her a Snow Cone from the ice cream truck just minutes before the alleged incident! She was only sent to her room because she threw a stick at her brother's head!

Before anyone could get too worked up about her angry output, Hannah began another series of letters, sweet as any sugar cookie. "DYR PYPIL," she wrote. "I LAV AVRYWON."

"DYR IDAHO," another said. "I WD LIK TO GO THAR."

It didn't take long, however, for her to return to her writergrrl roots. In a little heart-covered, pastel-papered notebook, she wrote more scathing critiques of her dad, and some of her brother. I somehow managed to escape her writerly wrath. "MOM," she wrote in her journal, "WY R YOU SO LAVEABL?" I knew I wouldn't be immune to her poison pen forever, but I enjoyed being the subject of these little tributes. Who needs good reviews when your own daughter writes, "THAT DANS WS GROOVY" and "MI MOM IS A POET. YOU CN TEL BCS OF HR BUKS"?

Hannah often sat on the couch, one leg crossed over the other like a stenographer from a forties movie, pencil and notebook in hand. She loved to write lists—"LOBSDR, FISH, SHRIMP, SHRK," "CHIKIN, TRKY, DAK, ROOSDR"—little inventories of the world she knows. She had her own "dictionary of bad words," which read "ASS ASS ASS HL." She seemed to know writing was a safe place to explore the taboo, to delve into rage and joy and the enchantment of the ordinary.

"I have my own way of spelling," Hannah said excitedly, as if she'd created her own civilization. When she'd ask how to spell something correctly, I'd tell her, but I loved the playful, fluid way she chose to spell words. I wanted to give her more time to swim around in her own language before she had to worry about spelling tests or red-pencil marks. Those would come soon enough.

I thought of Margaret Atwood's poem, "Spelling", in which she watches her daughter play with plastic letters on the floor and muses about how she was not just learning how to spell; she was also learning to make spells.

Hannah was learning to make spells, too.

Hannah and I never did have our sugar cookie spelling lesson. Our family polished off the container of treats like speed readers, spilling letter crumbs everywhere, before we could act out my plan. Anyway, Hannah had taught herself more than those cookies ever could.

The last page of Hannah's heart notebook read, in large letters, "I AM JIST FYN." Isn't that, ultimately, what we all try to say when we write? That we and our words are valid? That we deserve to be heard?

Later in the same poem, Atwood writes about how words create power when they're strung together. How beautiful to watch my daughter discover that power inside her. She helped me remember my own power as well, words sweet and biting, pungent and nourishing, in all of our fingers, on both of our tongues.

II

HYPERAERATION:
increased lung volume

thunder, thighs

I WAS BORN WITH TWISTED LEGS.

My feet were turned in, "pigeon-toed"; for the first six months of my life, I wore casts halfway up my shins, little stone booties to correct the tibial torsion. My legs still have a tendency to turn inward, especially when I'm feeling shy. My mind still has a tendency to turn toward my legs and cringe.

More than a decade ago, I decided to write a cultural history of the thigh, a book that would explore changing societal ideals, a book I hoped could help me make peace with my own thighs. As excited as I was by this project, it didn't coalesce for me, and I set it aside to focus on other writing projects. During our latest move, I came upon two thick binders: one full of thigh research, the other full of surveys I had circulated, asking women about their relationships with their legs.

I had forgotten how many women had responded.

I had forgotten how much thigh anxiety is out there in the world.

I used to have a happy relationship with my legs. I was a dancer and competitive figure skater as a girl, and the second-fastest runner in my class; my legs were sources of power and speed and grace. I could kick higher with my left leg, but I could lift my right leg higher in back (my signature move on the ice was to grasp my right leg behind me at the ankle and raise it up over my head). My legs shinnied me up trees, propelled me forward on bikes and in swimming pools, did the crab walk and the Hustle and carried me regularly up five flights of stairs to my apartment. My legs were my friends, my freedom. I didn't inspect them, couldn't imagine dividing my body into parts like a butcher cutting and grading meat.

The word "thigh" finds its root in the Indo-European teu, meaning "to swell." The very ampleness some of us worry about is written right into the etymology. Maybe if we remembered the word holds space for abundance, we'd be able to embrace it more fully in our own bodies.

The thighbone, or femur, is the longest bone in the human body. It finds its root in Latin—the outer thigh was known as the femar, the inner thigh the femen. The Latin word femina springs from the same root. The Romans considered thighs inherently female. Femina is also intimately connected with the Greek word phemi, meaning a woman's ability to speak with grace.

I never had a negative thought about my legs until I was thirteen. We had just moved, and I was feeling uncomfortable in my new house, uncomfortable with the way puberty was breathing down my neck. I wanted to outrun it, wanted to stay in a child's body forever.

"You have a long torso and short legs, huh?" a new friend said offhandedly one day as we stood outside our homeroom, taking off our winter boots.

"I guess so," I said, even though I had never noticed this before. I suddenly felt hideous, my upper body stretched to ghoulish lengths, my legs compressed into stubby nubs. I wanted to put my boots back on, put my jacket back on, put my scarf and my hat and my gloves back on so no one would be able to see my freakishness. My friend closed her locker and walked into the classroom humming, unaware.

Thigh anxiety appears to be a fairly recent phenomenon. The first evidence I've found of the thigh-hatred industry was a self-published diet booklet from 1953, "Special Diet for Fat Hips and Thighs." It was written by Ruth Pfahler, who owned a "reducing shop" in Decatur, Illinois. Her theory: "People with excess weight on hips and thighs consume too many sweets." This booklet aside, it appears widespread thigh anxiety didn't sweep the nation until the 1960s, with the advent of the miniskirt. It billowed into epidemic proportions in the 1970s, when French doctors coined the term "cellulite" in *Vogue* magazine, naming it a "disfiguring" disorder. Until then, cellulite had been considered a natural part of the female body, something 90 percent of us share. Liposuction was introduced in France in 1977 and came to the States in 1981. The 1980s also ushered in the fitness craze (not to mention bathing suits and leotards cut high on the hip), which added a whole new dimension to thigh anxiety. Wendy Stehling's book *Thin Thighs in 30 Days* was released in 1982; it sold more than 425,000 copies in less than two months.

I was in and out of the hospital with Crohn's disease much of my freshman year of high school. My mom brought a photo from one of my skating shows to my room so I could remember being out in the world, remember being well, and so my doctors could see me as a whole person, not just a patient. In it, I'm wearing a little white Spandex dress with strips of red sequins stitched into the shape of a bow tie and tuxedo lapels, a matching bowler on my head—the costume for my solo to "I Got Rhythm."

My gastroenterologist couldn't stop staring at my thighs in the photo, one stretched before me in a shallow lunge, my toe pick rooting me to the ice.

"They're like tree trunks," he marveled, spreading his white-coated arms. "They're each as big around as your waist."

I was mortified. I knew I had developed muscular thighs from skating, but I had never thought of them as weird before—just strong. After his comments, my thighs felt obscene to me, in the photo and in my body, even though much of that muscle had atrophied beneath my hospital gown. My mom tried to convince me the doctor had been showing admiration, but I didn't believe her. I was convinced my legs had been officially diagnosed as abnormal, wrong.

I recently came upon this photo; my quads are well developed in it but not dramatically so (and even if they had been, that shouldn't have been a problem). My doctor's words had managed to influence my long-term memory of the photograph, not to mention my long-term relationship with my legs. Words like his—whether careless or intentionally hurtful—can hover over our bodies like a distorted lens; they can make it hard for us to see, to appreciate what is truly there.

Survey Question #3: *Has anyone ever made a comment about your thighs? Your mother, a lover, a friend? What did they say? What was your response?*

"In high school, my mom would get mad at me for buying mini-skirts because, 'Your legs are so ugly, you should try to hide them.' She was raised in Taiwan and thinks Asian women are supposed to be thin and petite."

"My husband once mentioned that they look like bad Jell-O that contained some sort of bumpy fruit. I cried, he said, 'What did I say?,' and I had to leave the room and cover up."

"My paternal grandmother would poke at my thighs with her unlit cigarette, a chopstick, whatever was handy when I was a girl. She would tell me they were 'fat and lumpy, like an old woman.' I was VERY self-conscious in school because I was and am large and she always made me cry."

"I had a lover once who told me I had fat legs, so I told him he had a small prick, and we parted company."

My own boyfriend in high school once grabbed my legs and growled "meaty thighs" like a hungry beast; he meant it affectionately, but I couldn't help but shrink away from his hand. My boyfriend in college, who became my first husband, told me my legs were works of art, but I figured he just wasn't looking at them closely enough.

More than one-third of the women in my survey had been called "Thunder Thighs" at some point in their lives. Many were still haunted by this. None of us had reinterpreted "thunder" to mean "power."

After I went into remission and my body started to accept nutrition again, I shot up several inches, leaving long, red stretch marks on my upper thighs. They looked like talon marks, as if growth had to claw its way into my flesh. Of course, this made me all the more self-conscious about my legs.

"What happened to you?" a friend asked, aghast, that summer

when we changed into our bathing suits. The red streaks coursed down my thighs like runnels of lava. I couldn't answer her; all I could do was cry. She stared at me in disbelief. "Forget about it," she finally told me. "Jeez."

I couldn't forget about it. For several years, I couldn't talk about my body, any part of it, without crying. Every doctor's visit unleashed a torrent. Every conversation about periods made me dissolve. I reached a turning point my freshman year of college when I announced, heart pounding, "I haven't shaved my legs in ten days" to everyone in my dorm lobby. I was part of an alternative program within the university, so this was not a shocking confession—most women there were hairy legged, hairy pitted. It was a huge step for me, though; I was amazed that I could speak about my body—especially my legs—out loud, and the world didn't fall apart.

During the Victorian Era, it was considered improper, if not downright scandalous, to utter "thigh" out loud in mixed company. When chicken thighs were served, they were referred to as "dark meat" (a term that survives to this day.) And, of course, it was considered even more improper to show one's thighs during a time when even a peek of ankle could cause a scandal.

In college, I started to feel more at home in my body than I had in years—I was in the dance studio just about every day, was finding ways to weave my body into my writing, was having lots of sex—but two different bodyworkers told me my energy only radiated from my hips up; it was as if my brain was pretending my legs didn't exist, they said. One bodyworker spun her pendulum over my body and told me this was because of family pain from two generations back. This made some sense; my diabetic grandfather's legs had been amputated when my mom was a young woman. Perhaps I was experiencing the opposite of phantom limb, reliving my grandfather's experience in reverse—his brain could feel legs that weren't there; my brain wouldn't acknowledge legs that were.

Survey Question #8: *Do you think about your thighs during sex? If so, how does this affect your experience?*

"I do notice that if I'm feeling receptive, my thighs just naturally fall open…uh, like the petals of a beautiful flower unfolding. Yeah."

" Yes, I do. Because I have arthritis of the hips, I have a hard time opening my thighs, which means I can't have 'normal' sex, which means my love and I must get creative and work around the thighs."

"Occasionally, I'd be self-conscious when I got up to go to the bathroom but only with new partners."

"I so prefer my thighs by candlelight."

"A cartoon ran in *MAD Magazine* in the late eighties (possibly *National Lampoon*). It was about how naked you could expect 'chicks' to get based on their religion—the Reform Jewish girl would get as naked as her cellulite would allow and was depicted in a bra and half-slip."

"If I'm on top, I try to pull at the blankets on the bed, as if in some sort of fit of ecstasy, when I'm actually trying to cover some of my thighs and hips."

"Sometimes, in both good and bad ways. I think that I'm glad they're strong, that they feel good. That's a good thing. If I'm thinking they're fat, unattractive, dimpled...I'm probably not having good sex. Not a bad indicator."

❧

During my first pregnancy at twenty-two, I scrutinized my body's changes from month to month and noticed a little patch of cellulite on the back of one of my thighs, a little starburst of spider veins on the side of the other. I assumed they were temporary, that once I had the baby, things would smooth out, disappear, that my body would bounce back to its prepregnancy state as if nothing had happened, like memory foam. I didn't anticipate the way the cellulite would start to drift lightly down my thighs, didn't anticipate the way other little veins would burst forth, one in the shape of a mouth, a tiny kiss left on my skin, one I couldn't wipe away, no matter how hard I tried.

In labor, each contraction steered clear of my belly and back and seized the fronts of my thighs, my legs clenching so hard, aching so profoundly, they felt they might shatter. Leg labor, my midwife called it, as if my baby was going to be born through my quadriceps like Dionysus, sewn into Zeus's thigh after his pregnant mother's death; or like Aurva, who, according to the *Griffith Ramayana*, "issued from his mother's thigh with such lustre that he blinded his persecutors." Given my history with my legs, the fact that I ended up with leg labor—a pretty uncommon presentation—made a strange sort of sense.

❧

My family took a vacation to Jamaica when I was a baby; I consider two framed black-and-white photos from the trip amongst my most prized possessions—in one, my dad is doing the limbo; in the other, my mom is about to go under the stick, hips thrust forward in a mod, skirted bathing suit. When she saw the pictures on my bookshelf, she shook her head and said, "That's before I lost my legs." It seemed a strange thing to say for a woman whose dad's legs had been amputated. I felt an uncommon rush of protectiveness toward my own legs—I realized I didn't ever want to lose them; I told myself I would never take them for granted again. My mom must have noticed the horrified expression on my face at her comment, because she said, "It was before I lost the baby weight." The tenderness I had been feeling toward my thighs dissolved; I started to think about the weight I was still hoping to lose.

In what appears to be a highly unscientific—not to mention insult-ing—study done by L'eggs, 47 percent of women said they'd give up chocolate to have smoother legs; 25 percent would give up talking on the phone, and 18 percent would stop shopping. Thirty-one percent found cellulite more troublesome than their partner's bad behavior; 17 percent found it worse than dealing with their in-laws, and 23 percent feared cellulite more than turning into their own mother. Of course, this study was released at the same time as their L'eggs Care Anti-Cellulite Legwear. So many other companies have capitalized on the same consumer thigh angst—today, you can pay to have your thigh fat frozen, melted, wrapped, kneaded or vacuumed away (results not guaranteed); you can buy creams with caffeine and retinol and seaweed and quinoa and a host of other natural and chemical ingredients to smooth on your thighs in an attempt to smooth them out (results also not guaranteed).

My first husband's best friend visited shortly after my second baby was born, when I was twenty-five. He told me I was looking good, his eyes sweeping up and down; I just needed to work on my thighs, he said. He didn't know thighs were the Achilles' heel of my body image, didn't know how deeply his words would cut; even so, that gave him no right to say it. My body didn't owe him anything, not that I thought to tell him this. I didn't think to speak up for my thighs, which were providing a soft nest for my sleeping baby. I felt a hot rush of shame instead, as if I had committed some grave, moral offense by not living up to his idea of what a woman's thighs should look like. And, of course, that wasn't just his idea—he had seen that idea, that ideal on every billboard and magazine and sitcom and porn video and commercial and cardboard cutout of women advertising beer. So had I. I thought my thighs needed work, too.

❧

A curse from the Bible: "May the Lord cause your thigh to sag and your belly to distend; may this water that induces the spell enter your body, causing the belly to distend and the thigh to sag." (Num. 5:21)

Could this have been the beginning of men judging women's bodies? Could this be where women's thigh anxiety really began—fear of a vengeful God?

❧

I started wearing board shorts over my bathing suits, not wanting to inflict my thighs on the world, not wanting to hear anyone else talk about them. It didn't matter that my cellulite was only visible in certain light; it grew in my mind more than it did on my legs—over the years, the board shorts got longer and longer. Anytime I saw a woman with cellulite walk down the beach uncovered, I would admire her and her bravery. I thought about all the tabloid covers shaming stars who dared to show cellulite on the beach. I thought about hazing rituals I had heard of, in which fraternity boys draw "fat circles" around bulges on sorority pledges' thighs, marking their skin as a plastic surgeon would. I thought about an essay by a rock star in which he says something disparaging about a woman's cellulite, implying that the woman's partner must be disgusted by her; I thought about a review I had read of a photography exhibit, where the male critic had called photos of a woman with cellulite "grotesque." I thought about how my mom covered up all the parts of her body she didn't like, especially her neck, never going out in public without a scarf. *Cover up your imperfections,* I learned from her. *Obsess about your imperfections. Don't let anyone know you aren't smooth and sleek as a seal.*

In ancient Egypt, the Goddess Hathor—also known as the Celestial Cow—had legs that held up the sky. Women would pray to have big, powerful thighs like Hathor's, in both this life and beyond. One papyrus is translated as "(Hathor) shall make thy thighs large among the goddesses, she shall open thine eye so that thou shalt see each day."

I wrote my first book, *Fruitflesh: Seeds of Inspiration for Women Who Write,* to try to help myself and other women reclaim our bodies, tap into our bodies as sources of deep creativity and power. I wish I could say that after writing this book, I never felt bad about my body again, that writing this book helped me forever embrace every inch of myself unceasingly, unfailingly.

We often teach what we need to learn; sometimes we need to learn the same thing over and over again. I do have long, sweet stretches when I feel at home in my skin, when I don't care what other people think about how I look, when I'm able to view my body with compassion and kindness and gratitude. But two decades after writing the book, there are still times when I backslide, times when I look at the mirror and cringe, times when I reach for the board shorts, times when I freeze if my husband, Michael, touches my thigh, sure his hand is measuring it, judging it.

And he's not. He's not measuring; he's not judging. He loves every part of me; he doesn't understand why I sometimes flinch if he takes a playful peek up the back of my skirt, why I feel convinced he's trying to block my thighs from his sight if he holds on to them in bed.

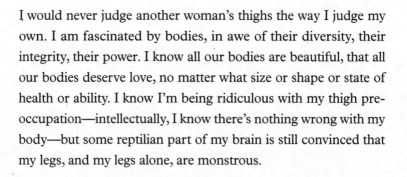

I would never judge another woman's thighs the way I judge my own. I am fascinated by bodies, in awe of their diversity, their integrity, their power. I know all our bodies are beautiful, that all our bodies deserve love, no matter what size or shape or state of health or ability. I know I'm being ridiculous with my thigh preoccupation—intellectually, I know there's nothing wrong with my body—but some reptilian part of my brain is still convinced that my legs, and my legs alone, are monstrous.

The Anxiety and Depression Association of America describes body dysmorphic disorder as "a body-image disorder characterized by persistent and intrusive preoccupations with an imagined or slight defect in one's appearance.

"People with BDD can dislike any part of their body, although they often find fault with their hair, skin, nose, chest, or stomach. In reality, a perceived defect may be only a slight imperfection or nonexistent. But for someone with BDD, the flaw is significant and prominent, often causing severe emotional distress and difficulties in daily functioning."

Supposedly only 1 percent of the population suffers from BDD, but I'm guessing a larger percentage has a mild case. We're practically bred to have BDD in our culture. It's never been diagnosed, but I wouldn't be surprised if I have a touch of BDD; it doesn't affect me on a daily basis, and the distress it causes is not particularly severe, but it is definitely a "persistent and intrusive preoccupation," and I know I see my thighs as if I'm looking at them in a fun house mirror, each flaw, each billow magnified. If you met me, you probably wouldn't notice my thighs; you probably wouldn't understand why I'd feel compelled to write an essay—to have considered writing a whole book—on the subject. I barely understand it myself; I only know I need to face my own, unreasonable fixations, find a way to bring them to light.

❧

Thigh anxiety is definitely a first-world problem, and largely a white problem. Black and Latinx cultures still tend to see big, powerful legs as sexy. Missy Elliott celebrates her thick thighs in several of her songs, and Pitbull's praise of Ciara's generous thighs in "That's How I'm Feeling' " is worlds away from Robert Plant wailing that a woman with big legs has no soul. Even so, BIPOC women are developing eating disorders and body-image crises at an alarming rate.

In *Wanting to Be Her: Body Image Secrets Victoria Won't Tell You,* Michelle Graham interviews Sandra, a woman from San Juan, Puerto Rico. "I remember my pride at being complimented for my piernas gordas like my mother," Sandra says. When she went off to college, Sandra was faced with a different beauty standard; she internalized this and "started a war against my 'big' butt and thighs...too flaca in the barrio, too gorda downtown."

The Thigh Gap Hack: The Shortcut to Slimmer, Feminine Thighs Every Woman Secretly Desires was written by a Black woman, a fact that distresses Veronica Wells, who wrote the essay "Do Black Girls Want a Thigh Gap?" at *MadameNoire*. She ends with, "For those of you still lamenting the fact that there's not a gap between your thighs, let me leave you with this. According to my grandmother, the most important function of thick thighs is to keep your 'fishy' warm. And that's important."

⁂

In 2014, I needed to have several inches of obstructed intestine, a complication from Crohn's disease, removed. I had been unwell for months, unable to eat more than a couple of bites of food at a time without writhing in pain, and my weight had dropped to the point where people were expressing alarm. In the hospital, I fell beneath one-hundred pounds, becoming so weak, I could barely stand. My ass was gone, my legs spindles, but I somehow found myself scared to put on weight as I recovered; I found myself wearing my flimsiest shoes to doctor appointments to keep the numbers on the scale low, my thinking around my weight having grown distorted, disordered.

As I regained strength and health, my senses about this thankfully also returned. I started eating with gusto again, with pleasure. I gained back all the weight I'd lost during the hospitalization, and then some. Some of the clothes that fell off of me when I was at my tiniest turned snug; I tried not to care about this. I tried to focus less on my physical appearance, more on my physical experience, grateful for the thighs that let me groove across the dance studio and walk the trail behind our house and squat down to play with my son and pull my husband in closer. The thighs that keep my fishy warm.

~~❧~~

Studies have shown we spend an average of six and a half years of our life worrying. It's embarrassing to think about how much time I've wasted worrying about my thighs. Time I could have spent writing, or agitating for change, or using my legs to do something fun. And that's been the aim of beauty standards all along, right? To get women to spend money on unnecessary products and procedures, to get us to spend time worrying about our thighs or our bellies or our wrinkles or our breasts when we could be speaking up for our rights or making art or otherwise kicking ass. That's not a system I want to perpetuate. As comedian Sarah Silverman says, "Mother Teresa didn't walk around complaining about her thighs. She had shit to do." I have shit to do, too. When I start to worry about my thighs now, I try (not always successfully) to redirect that energy in a more positive direction—channel it into a poem or a petition or a dance, or even just renewed appreciation for all my thighs can do. It appears that's what therapy for body dysmorphic disorder often entails, using "cognitive restructuring" to help patients recognize and shift irrational thinking patterns. If I'm unable to do this sustainably on my own, I'll find someone who can help.

I see how women are helping one another online now, much in the way I had hoped to with my thigh-book project. A hashtag on Twitter, #thighreading, started when @princess_labia posted a photo of her thighs after she realized "they could tell a story, the way my palms could tell a story." In an interview with *The Today Show*, she says, "My thighs are something I've been insecure about my entire life. We don't ever really see thighs that aren't retouched and that are of average size." Since then, women have been posting photos of their own thighs, using her hashtag, sharing their stretch marks and cellulite and scars from surgery and self-harm, with tweets like @mxurakate's "#thighreading helps so much. I didn't realize that so many other people have stretch marks wow now I feel like a normal human being" and @LyssaLatte's "#thighreading I've always said my thighs look like raw hamburger meat cuz of cellulite. I should be easier on myself." If #thighreading, or tv shows like *Orange Is the New Black*, which show women of all sizes, or *So You Think You Can Dance*, where so many of the dancers have big, strong thighs like mine, or even the phrase "thick thighs save lives," popularized in 2016 by model Ashley Graham, had existed when I was thirteen, or even twenty-five, I doubt my thigh loathing would have become as deeply entrenched in my psyche.

Survey Question #9: *If your thighs could talk, what would they tell you?*

- "You're kind of hard on us, don't you think? So we don't look like supermodel thighs, so what? Hey, look at Diana Ross. Cut us some slack, sister. We never hear you complaining when you're biking up those long hills."
- "For crying out loud, get off your lazy ass and take us for a walk already!"
- "Don't worry too much about us; we're cool. We aren't going anywhere, and we will never look the way you wished we did—so give it up."
- "Quit wearing those tight, tummy-trimmer underwear from Sears. We can't breathe!
- "Rub me."
- "Keep on truckin'."

- "Spread us more frequently. Do it for the team."
- "Lighten the fuck up."
- "LOVE US!"

My dear friend and mentor, poet and novelist Alma Luz Villanueva, had responded to my original survey with great verve (in answer to my question "What do your thighs like to wear?" she had responded "THE OCEAN"), and years later sent a follow-up: "I've always loved my thighs because they're strong and guide me through the world," she told me. "I trust my loyal, *amiga* thighs, their tender strength...*QUE VIVA LAS THIGHS*!!"

QUE VIVA LAS THIGHS, indeed.

I have an image in my head of all the people who've ever had negative thoughts about our thighs coming together; I imagine us shedding our board shorts, shedding our shame, and creating a giant kick line. Not like the Rockettes, who all have similarly-shaped thighs—this would be a diverse kick line, with thighs of every size and age and color and ability and gender identity; dimpled thighs, smooth thighs, muscled thighs, partial thighs, thighs with stretch marks and scars and veins and track marks and bruises and wrinkles and tattoos and other histories, hard and sweet, written on our skin. Some of us can kick way up over our heads; some of us can kick knee-high, some join the line sitting or lying down, but all of us are dancing in our own way; all of us are celebrating our bodies just as they are.

You can see it, can't you, this glorious line of dancers?

All our arms linked together?

All our thighs, thundering?

the women
who helped

WHEN I'VE TOLD THIS STORY IN THE PAST, I'VE focused on two things:

1. I was assaulted in a movie theater.
2. When I tried to report the crime, the police officer convinced me it would be embarrassing to have my name associated with such a case.

Sometimes, when I've told this story, I've given details: It was a ten p.m. movie. I went by myself, taking a break from studying (it was 1987; I was nineteen, a sophomore in college). The movie starred Kiefer Sutherland; the love interest was deaf; the title included the word "Moon." I was wearing an orange-and-yellow hippie poncho that still smelled musty, like the thrift store where I had purchased it. My hair was in a ponytail. A man sat directly behind me in an otherwise empty theater. This felt weird, but I figured he was lonely and wanted to be close to another human being. I turned my head slightly and smiled. I couldn't see him but wanted him to know I knew he was there. Later, I wondered whether he had taken this as an invitation. When I first felt one of my hairs snap, I thought a strand had gotten stuck between my body and the chair. Then another hair snapped, then another—*pop pop pop pop*. Before I could make sense of what was happening, my head was yanked violently backward, then yanked and yanked and yanked and yanked by the ponytail, as if the man was trying to pull my head straight off my neck. I don't recall screaming, but I must have screamed. In my state of shock and confusion and pain, I realized the man was pleasuring himself with my hair. Somehow, I got away. I can remember the sticky floor as I reeled down the row of seats, the way each foot made a kissing sound as it lifted.

When I worked up the nerve to call the police from my dorm room later that night, after a long, long, shower, followed by a bath because I still didn't feel clean, the officer laughed and said, "You don't want your name attached to a masturbation case, now, do you?" I found myself flooded with shame, flooded with tears, my throat closing before I hung up the phone.

When I've told this story, I've focused on these two men—the man in the theater, and the police officer who shut me down. I realize I've left something out when I've related this story, maybe the most important part.

I've left out the women.

I've left out the woman who said, "Oh, honey, what happened?" after I flopped onto the floor of my dorm lobby, shaking and crying, having crawled through the back window that was always left open after the front door was locked for the night. I probably wouldn't have told anyone if she hadn't been there and seen me in that state.

I've left out the woman who called the movie theater and said, "A man did a really disgusting thing to my friend. Could you check and see if he's still there, and call the police if he is?" (He wasn't.)

I've left out the woman who told me, "What doesn't kill you makes you stronger," a ubiquitous quote, of course, one I have a complicated relationship with now but one I had never heard before, one that truly did help at the time.

I've left out the woman who walked me to the counseling office on campus the next morning.

I've left out the counselor who listened, who gently guided me toward my own inner counsel with her voice.

I've left out the women who cheered me on when I made the decision not to cut off my hair, not to give that man such power over my body.

I've left out the women, who, after they heard what happened, told me their own stories of assault. One by one, they came up to me and said, "Me, too," "Me, too," "Me, too," ushering me into a world I had previously been shielded from—a disturbing world in which so many women had been violated; a powerful world in which women support one another.

And I wonder how I could have left these women out of my story, how I could have given all my attention to the two men who had traumatized me instead of the many women who had helped. "Look for the helpers," Mr. Rogers told us, but I didn't have to look for them in 1987—they found me, these women, and I am so deeply grateful for all of them, many of whom I had barely known before the night of the assault. I wish I had acknowledged them sooner. When I tell this story in the future, this constellation of women will light the way.

we too

(women writing the first-person plural)

W E, THE WOMEN WHO WRITE IN FIRST-PERSON plural, come to this point of view from different angles. We want to speak for a group. We want to show the danger of groupthink. We want to feel solidarity. We want to expose fracture. We want to try something new. We find it's the only way to tell the story we want or need to tell.

We hold these truths to be self-evident that not all of us are created societally equal. That this inequality is built into, perpetuated by the language itself. That women and nonbinary people should not have to fall under the label "men." That the first-person plural can be a way to tell the truths we hold.

In 2004, journalist Laura Miller wrote, "The communal inclinations of women, though often praised, are riddled with ambivalence, and that makes the first-person plural a particularly fraught choice for women writers," but our choice isn't always fraught, our inclinations not always riddled with widespread ambivalence (at least, not enough so to sway us). She wrote this long before more women started speaking out en masse, through hashtag, through political campaigns, through bodies on the street. Rather than fraught, we've found the first-person plural can be fierce. It can be freeing. Sometimes it can even be fun.

"There was something joyous, almost ecstatic, about the 'we' voice," Julie Otsuka said of her novel *The Buddha in the Attic* in a *Poets & Writers* profile. "I think of it being more like a song."

Some of us come to the choral voice because we know heroes aren't always singular, know that the idea of the individual hero (most traditionally, the individual *male* hero) has led to so many silenced stories. We want to give voice to silenced stories, want to expand the idea of what a story can be and who can tell it.

"In Heaven, we are used to treating our girlhood like a territory that must be defended, staving off intruders and fending off disasters with each strategically plotted move," writes Mathangi Subramanian in her novel *A People's History of Heaven*, which revolves around a group of girls—queer, straight, Hindu, Muslim, Christian—banding together to save their neighborhood from developers in Bangalore, India. "In our mothers' eyes, in our eyes, it's a war we have a chance of winning."

Besides, we know the individual is a myth. We are made of about 37 trillion cells. About 100 trillion microorganisms live on and in our bodies. The breath we inhale has been exhaled by other humans and animals and plants. We are what we eat, all that nourishment and toxicity. The dust that coats our windowsills, our bookshelves is made up of so much dead skin, so much shed hair, all of us mingled together.

We like to think of aspen groves, the way each tree may look separate but is part of a collective organism, tangled underground. We like to think of murmurations, flocks of birds swooping around as one, or maybe schools of fish swimming together to scare off predators.

In her 1983 review of Joan Chase's *During the Reign of the Queen of Persia*, Margaret Atwood categorizes the novel, narrated by cousins (two pairs of sisters), as being "concerned with the female matrix."

"A matrix is both what we spring from and what we are

embedded in," she writes, "and the 'we' cannot decide which definition applies."

We're all concerned with the female matrix, with where we spring from, where we're embedded. Some of our characters try to climb out of this bed; some of them burrow in deeper (and some, like the Orthodox Jewish women in Tova Mirvis' *The Ladies Auxiliary*, try to get out but get sucked right back in):

"When we were teenagers, we would imagine that when we had daughters of our own, we wouldn't be so strict. We would give them room to explore, let them decide for themselves if they wanted to follow this way of life. But once we were in the parental role, it wasn't as simple. We wanted our daughters to grow up and get married, to have Jewish homes and raise Jewish families. We wanted them to pass on this tradition to their children and to their children's children. We didn't want them to be exposed to bad influences, ones that might make them steer from this path that had been set out for them since birth. We wanted them to avoid the confusion of the modern world, where no one seemed to believe in anything anymore. We wanted them to always feel rooted in their tradition, to be close to their families, their community, and God. And we didn't know how to do that if we made no ground rules, set down no boundaries."

We set and trample boundaries in our stories. We're a Greek chorus offering commentary, sounding the alarm. We're a Puerto Rican–American chorus, a Japanese-immigrant chorus, a WASP-American chorus, a Black chorus, an Orthodox Jewish chorus in a small, Southern town, a chorus of girls in India, a chorus of Hungarian ghosts. We imagine ourselves a charm of foxes. A shrewdness of apes. A parliament of owls.

In her 2004 article, Laura Miller also noted, "for male writers, the collective narrator is most often on the outside trying to peep in—usually at a woman or women—but female writers speak from the center of the mystery." This is not true of all of us—some of us choose to peep a story from its margins—but we do love the mystery of the collective, the contradictions and connections it holds.

Some of us narrate our works entirely in the first-person plural. Others among us allow individual voices to rise from the group to speak for themselves now and then; others punctuate the "we" voice throughout a more traditionally told narrative. Jaquira Díaz does this in *Ordinary Girls,* threading the first-person plural experience of her group of friends throughout her primarily first-person memoir: "It was the same the next summer, and the summer after that: we went right back to drinking, smoking, fighting, dancing dancing dancing, running away. We wanted to be seen finally, to exist in the lives we'd mapped out for ourselves We wanted more than noise—we wanted everything. We were ordinary girls but we would've given anything to be monsters. We weren't creatures or aliens or women in disguise, but girls. We were girls."

"We were girls once," say Brit Bennett's older church ladies, whose first-person plural judgment and wisdom pepper the multiple POV, close third person narrative of Bennett's novel *The Mothers.* "We would have told her that all together, we got centuries on her. If we laid all our lives toe to heel, we were born before the Depression, the Civil War, even America itself."

Margaret Atwood uses the first-person plural in part of her novel and stage play, *The Penelopiad*—while most of the characters speak singularly, Penelope's maids, who were hanged, speak as one. (An aside: one of us—okay, me, okay, *I*—hadn't heard of *The Penelopiad* until I mentioned my then-forthcoming book, narrated collectively by ghosts of the victims of Countess Bathory, when I was teaching at a women's poetry workshop in Malawi, and one of my brilliant co-teachers, TJ Dema, said, "Oh, like *The Penelopiad*." I was intrigued but nervous, worried my work would seem derivative, even though I had never read this particular work by Atwood. I downloaded *The Penelopiad* in play form on my phone and read it on the flight home; I was relieved that her work was wildly different from my own book, although there was one scene, where Atwood's Maids recount moments of stolen comfort—"Between the bright hall and the dark scullery we crammed filched meat into our mouths. We laughed together in our attics, in our nights. We snatched what we could"—that was strikingly similar to a moment in my own book. But I tried not to freak out. I tried to think of it as cool that Atwood and I had tapped into the same stream. Collective consciousness is real, right? It's what drives the first-person plural voice we've chosen to use.)

We've heard about the "royal we," and some of our characters, like the fifties housewives of Kate Walbert's *Our Kind*, are indeed born into privilege. Many, maybe most, of our characters, however, come from far less prosperous, and often marginalized communities. To quote Brit Bennett's church mothers again: "We tried to love the world. We cleaned after this world, scrubbed its hospital floors and ironed its shirts, sweated in its kitchens and spooned school lunches, cared for its sick and nursed its babies. But the world didn't want us, so we left and gave our love to Upper Room. Now we're afraid of this world. A boy snatched Hattie's purse one night and now none of us go out after dark. We hardly go anywhere at all, besides Upper Room. We've seen what this world has to offer. We're scared of what it wants."

Some of our collective characters have a wild mix of backgrounds, bound together by circumstance, as in *The Wives of Los Alamos*, by TaraShea Nesbit: "We were European women born in Southampton and Hamburg, Western women born in California and Montana, East Coast women born in Connecticut and New York, Midwestern women born in Nebraska and Ohio, or Southern women from Mississippi or Texas, and no matter who we were we wanted nothing to do with starting all over again, and so we paused, we exhaled, and we asked, *What part of the Southwest?* Our husbands muttered, *I don't know.* And we thought that was strange."

Sometimes our choice to write in the collective voice feels

strange or mysterious to us, even as it also feels perfect for our project. "The decision (to write first-person plural) was intuitive at first," Laura Lippman said in an interview about her novel *The Most Dangerous Thing*, "that is, I knew it was right, without knowing why it was right. When I finished the book, I realized that these passages are a consensual version of what happened in the past, that the survivors have agreed on what happened and that's why the story is, at turns, unflattering to each of them. They are working out their level of culpability in several tragedies and they just can't face this alone."

Sometimes we weave our process into the narrative, create a meta-intention for our choice of point of view:

From Andrea Barrett's *The Air We Breathe*: "If the voice we've made to represent all of us seems to speak from above, or from the grave, and pretends to know what we can't, exactly, know—what Miles was thinking, what Naomi meant—that's our way of doing penance. Singly, we failed to shelter Leo. Singly, then, we've forbidden ourselves to speak. *This is what happened,* we say together. *This— this!—is what we did.*'"

From Eleanor Brown's *The Weird Sisters*: "We all have stories we tell ourselves. We tell ourselves we are too fat, or too ugly, or too old, or too foolish. We tell ourselves these stories because they allow us to excuse our actions and they allow us to pass off the responsibilities for things we have done, maybe for something within our control, but anything other than the decisions we have made...There are times in our lives that we have to realize that our past is precisely what it is and we cannot change it. But we can change the story we tell ourselves about it, and by doing that, we can change the future."

"We" can be a family, a couple, a group of friends, a class (school or socioeconomic), a gender identity, a workplace, a community. We can be small and painfully insular; we can be large and contain multitudes.

Of course, we know the word "we" can never include every-one. Look at "We, the People"; think of all the people the writers of this phrase excluded. We sometimes weave such exclusion into our narratives. When there is a "we," there is usually also a "not we," sometimes an oppressive or oppressed "them."

Julie Otsuka plays with this to powerful effect in *The Buddha in the Attic,* starting with one "we"—"picture brides" coming to America from Japan ("On the boat we were mostly virgins. We had long black hair and flat wide feet and we were not very tall. Some of us had eaten nothing but rice gruel as young girls and had slightly bowed legs, and some of us were only fourteen years old and were still young girls ourselves")—and ending with another "we," a "we" who sees these women as "them," a "we" complicit in sending these women to internment camps. ("The Japanese have disappeared from our town. Their houses are boarded up and empty now.")

We can use "we" to expose such injustice; we can also use "we" as a powerful rallying cry, a call to action, a way to speak collectively against power. Think of protest chants:

"What do we want?"
"Peace!"
"When do we want it?"
"Now!"

In the Wachowski sisters' Netflix series *Sense8*, Nomi—a trans woman character played by trans actor Jamie Clayton—says she's joining a Pride march to remember she's not only a "me"; she's also a "we."

Collective voice can lead to collective action, collective transformation.

In her introduction to *Whose Story is This?*, Rebecca Solnit writes, "We are building something immense together that, though invisible and immaterial, is a structure, one we reside within—or, rather, many overlapping structures. They're assembled from ideas, visions and values emerging out of conversations, essays, editorials, arguments, slogans, social-media messages, books, protests, and demonstrations. About race, class, gender, sexuality; about nature, power, climate, the interconnectedness of all things; about compassion, generosity, collectivity, communion; about justice, equality, possibility. Though there are individual voices and people who got there first, these are collective projects that matter not when one person says something but when a million integrate it into how they see and act in the world. The we who inhabits those structures grows as what was once subversive or transgressive settles in as normal, as people outside the walls wake up one day inside them and forget they were ever anywhere else."

When we write "we," we can create "we." We can reach beyond what can feel like the terrible isolation of the first-person singular and find a wider voice. A "We, the People" of our own making.

her shadow

(or, a portrait of my mother through other daughters' portraits of their mothers)

"Reading other daughters' accounts…I sometimes feel we are all the daughters of the same mythical mother… .While I am reading these other daughters' accounts, their mothers become my mother."

—*Edwidge Danticat, The Art of Death*[1]

"I AM THE QUEEN OF SHEBA," MY MOTHER announced to me in a regal voice.[2]

You could say that my life as her daughter, the life of my imagination, began with my mother's visions. My sisters and I took them as our texts.[3] Thanks to my mother, I was raised to have a morbid imagination.[4]

I wanted to make my mother happy, that should come as no surprise. She had desires, for a harp, for seasonal seats at the opera.… From my mother I learned that truth is bendable, that what you wish is every bit as real as what you are.[5]

My mother wasn't perfect. My mother was intense. Things

---

1 Danticat, Edwidge. *The Art of Death*. Minneapolis: Graywolf Press, 2017.
2 Lyden, Jacki. *Daughter of the Queen of Sheba*. Boston: Houghton Mifflin, 1997.
3 *ibid.*
4 Tan, Amy. *The Opposite of Fate*. London: Penguin Books, 2004.
5 Slater, Lauren. *Lying*. New York: Random House, 2000.

didn't happen because they were possible, they happened because she decided they would.[6] She took the ought to be for the actual and adhered to what she should like and how things should be. It was as though she traveled by a map of the wrong place, hitting walls, driving into ditches, missing her destination but never stopping or throwing out the map. And she never stopped being Cinderella and told her own story largely as a series of things that happened to her rather than things she did.[7]

My mother's flair for drama always caught me off guard.[8] I said nothing though. I felt to speak would be to betray my mother.[9] My mother wanted always to be above reproach.[10]

I could never recreate myself as completely as my mother had.... I would fly home to...discover my mother in a new guise: a millionairess or a coronated duchess, a CEO patenting great inventions, a racehorse owner.[11]

At times my mother would go into obsessive monologues about our tragedies, about the curse, punctuating with her laments every bite we took.[12] I retreated inward. I couldn't deny that I did still have feelings of anger toward my mother.[13]

It occurred to me that maybe my mother could just turn this illness thing on and off at will—transmutation at her fingertips. Snap and she could be misdiagnosed or terminal. Seductress or victim.[14] Because of my mother's moods, I lived in a state of high suspense.[15]

My mother had been touched by death; it was no stranger to

6 Spiegelman, Nadja. *I'm Supposed to Protect You From All of This.* New York: Riverhead, 2016.
7 Solnit, Rebecca. *The Faraway Nearby.* New York: Viking, 2013.
8 Williams, Terry Tempest. *Refuge.* New York: Pantheon, 2000.
9 Slater (n 5)
10 Jarrell, Andrea. *I'm the One Who Got Away.* Berkeley: She Writes Press, 2017.
11 Lyden (n 2)
12 Tan (n 4)
13 Sexton, Linda Gray. *Searching for Mercy Street.* Boston: Little, Brown, & Co, 1994.
14 Gore, Ariel. *The End of Eve.* Portland: Hawthorne Books, 2014.
15 Tan (n 4)

her. There was no way to undo that, no way to make death forget her name.[16]

...my mother wrote no note, made no phone calls. She did not reach out for help or rescue, and she chose a method far more certain than her old routine of sleeping pills.... . She wanted to die, and her desire came not from anger but from despair.[17]

Please help me let go of this story. Please help me to give my heart over to my mother.[18]

For I could not be sure whether for the rest of my life I would be able to tell when it was really my mother and when it was really her shadow standing between me and the rest of the world.[19]

16 Smith, Tracy K. *Ordinary Light*. New York, Knopf, 2015.
17 Sexton (n 13)
18 Smith (n 16)
19 Kincaid, Jamaica. *Annie John*. New York: FS&G, 1997.

III
PONOPNEA:
painful breathing

get me away from here, i'm dying

ON CHRISTMAS EVE, I ARRANGE THE CARROT STICKS on half of my mother-in-law's narrow, scalloped dish, stack pale ribs of celery on the other side.

Last time.

The phrase echoes through me every few seconds—last time, last time—as I nestle large black olives into the curves around the edge of the dish, drape whole green onions over the top, balance some radishes in between. As I add a couple of ice cubes to keep everything cool and crisp.

Last time, last time, last time.

This has been my job at my mother-in-law's for the last twenty Christmas Eves: arranging the crudités into an intricate vegetable Jenga. It always feels like serious work. It always feels like art.

Like love.

Last time.

I am leaving my husband on New Year's Day. The new house is rented, the boxes half packed. The beginning of a trial separation I know in my heart will be permanent. Everyone knows, but no one says a word—not my husband's mother or sisters or their significant others; not our kids, not my husband. Certainly not me.

Christmas Eve goes on—my mother-in-law dumps the clear plastic tub of oysters and their brine into a copper pot along with some cream; she rubs the usual garlic clove along the inside of the salad bowl, takes the wide loaves of moist, dense, delicious bread—from dough she whips with a spoon rather than kneads—from the oven.

Last time. Last time. Last time. Last time.

My mother-in-law has become more of a mother to me than my own, especially in the fourteen years since my daughter's birth, when my mom's delusional disorder first surfaced. I watch her pour a glass of white wine, her jet-black Louise Brooks hair falling forward into her face, and love her so fiercely, so desperately, my chest aches. I'd waited so long to ask for a separation partly because I didn't want to separate from her.

Last time.

She usually makes a pot of Christmas borscht to accommodate me, her Ukrainian, Jewish vegetarian daughter-in-law, but this year, she's made split pea. It bubbles and snaps on the stove next to the oyster stew. "I thought I'd try something new," she says, but I imagine it's her way of starting to pull away from me, to loosen me from her heart.

After dinner (last time) and buttery, jam-filled cookies (last time) and the distributing of presents under the tinsel-dripping tree (last time), the instruments come out. My husband's family is a musical one; their gatherings often involve guitars and piano, sometimes fiddle and accordion. The usual carols are played, along with some bluegrass songs that give them a chance to harmonize; then the grown-ups retreat to the kitchen to clean up, and my seventeen-year-old son starts to strum Belle and Sebastian.

I'm a bit embarrassed to admit I had never heard of Belle and Sebastian until I saw the movie *High Fidelity*, and then I thought they were a made-up band, a fictional excuse for Jack Black to lose his shit. It wasn't until my kids became fans that I realized they were an actual group. If it weren't for my kids, I'd probably still be listening to Prince and the Talking Heads on a nearly exclusive basis.

I help wash the gold-trimmed stemware my mother-in-law inherited from her mother, almost the exact same set my mom inherited from hers. I find myself violently gripping each goblet, and I'm not sure if it's because I don't want to let them go or because I want to crush them with my hands.

My son launches into "Get Me Away from Here, I'm Dying." The song sounds so peppy, but the lyrics slay me, even though I don't catch most of them, just the title phrase and "You're so naive" and "I always cry at endings." That's enough. I set down the glass, tear off my yellow rubber gloves, run to my mother-in-law's TV room and wail. Deep, subterranean sounds that rip through me and seem to last for hours. No one comes in to check on me, no one asks if I'm okay after I finally emerge, embarrassed, my eyes completely red. They all love me but not enough to forgive what I'm about to do. When we're walking to the car though, my husband's older sister pulls me aside and gestures to her leopard-print coat. "I bought this for myself when I knew I had to leave my ex," she says, then wraps her arms around me. I start to cry all over again, tears matting the fake fur.

I always cry at endings.

∿

The first weeks of the separation, I feel as if I'm falling through space. Our shared circle of friends has tightened around my husband, and I am careening out of orbit, into someplace vast and dark and cold. I have taken to crying at night in huge, jagged sobs that make my face fall asleep, make my body disappear. Still, when I catch myself in the mirror, I am surprised at how the whites of my eyes look—clearer and brighter than I've ever seen them.

A friend leaves a ritual-in-a-bag on my doorstep. I am to cast a circle of salt, put a figure eight made of ribbon in the center, my name in one loop, my husband's in the other. I am to eat a blood orange, taste the sour and sweet together on my tongue. I am to take the scissors and cut the eight in half, severing what I thought would be infinite. I sob some more but feel the release of it, the light creeping back, as I wish each newly separate circle well.

New circles form. Love rushes in. Life enters the space blasted open by all that crying. I find out I'm pregnant at forty-one, nineteen years since my first pregnancy. I find myself saying, "I do."

I rest in bed with my two-day-old son and listen to my sister and my new husband whisper in the hallway outside the closed door. I can't make out what they're saying, but I know it has to do with my mom. They are trying to keep her away from me, to keep me and the baby in a protective bubble inside the room where he was born. I nuzzle my nose against his new head and breathe in his raw, sweet scent.

My mom has had delusional "episodes," as my family has taken to calling them—undiagnosed, untreated—on and off for almost sixteen years now but nothing like this. When she picked my sister up at the airport the day before, she had a flannel nightgown wrapped around her nose and mouth, a barrier against the poison she thought was coming through the vents. A Jack in the Box cup full of pee in the cup holder that she planned to have tested to see what drugs my dad had sprayed at her from his cell phone. When she held the baby for the first time yesterday and he immediately fell asleep, she was sure she had gassed him from the fumes lingering on her clothes.

My older kids come to meet their baby brother, and I venture out of the dim bedroom to have dinner with them; the table is covered with aluminum take-out containers full of red sauce–heavy pasta delivered by the local pizza place. My mom is still wearing the same purple turtleneck and black pants she had on yesterday and looks disheveled and sweaty; disconcerting, as she normally takes great pains with her appearance. Her eyes look different than usual, too: beady and dark. After we eat, she corners my nineteen-year-old and tells him she'll give him one hundred dollars to drive her to her friend's house in Carlsbad, an hour and a half away. She doesn't tell him she's scared to take her own car because she thinks it's being followed by numerous Middle Eastern men, a ghastly racism uncharacteristic of her. She doesn't tell him she's been driving as if she's in *The Bourne Identity* to escape them. He agrees—he has to study for an exam, but who wouldn't want a quick hundred dollars? When my mom goes to the bathroom, my sister and husband swoop in to give him the scoop. His face drops.

"I'm sorry, Nana," he says when she returns. "If we leave now, I won't be back until eleven, and I have a lot of homework."

My mom immediately charges toward my sister. "Sabotage!" she yells, one arm in the air as if she's rattling a saber. My husband steps in between them.

"We're going to a hotel," he says firmly. He had taken her to a hotel three nights ago after she showed up at our house unexpectedly, a cushion from an outdoor chaise under her arm so she could sleep on our floor, and she and I got into a shouting match. I went into labor a few hours later. "You can't come into my house and talk to people like that." My husband's face and voice both sharpen; I've never seen him like this. The papa bear in him rising up, protecting his clan. It's both terrifying and exhilarating.

My mom grabs my sister's batik scarf, the one my sister bought during a trip to Sausalito with an ex-boyfriend many years ago, and throws it over her head.

"You don't know how dangerous this is for me," she says, her entire face covered, then races out the door into a world where she thinks she's being chased and drugged and conspired against.

For a moment, we're all silent. It's as if she's pulled all the oxygen out of the house behind her. "Fuuuck," I say under my breath, not a word that often comes through me. We all stare at one another, eyebrows raised, reeling. Then my son points to my arms and says, "Look! A baby!" and everyone laughs, and the oxygen whooshes back in.

The rest of the night feels like a party. The kids start messing with instruments. My son puts on my daughter's blue Snuggie and looks like some sort of spirited monk as he plays guitar, swaying wildly in his chair. My sister and I sit side by side on the piano bench, laughing so hard, I'm worried the stitches in my perineum will pop. Then he starts to play "Get Me Away from Here, I'm Dying," and she and I turn to one another and burst into tears.

"What if that's the last image we ever have of her?" I ask, and we fall into each other, the baby nestled between us.

A few days later, we get a call from the coroner's office.

For weeks, I can't get the Belle and Sebastian song out of my head. I still only know those three lines: "Get me away from here, I'm dying," "You're so naïve," "I always cry at endings," but they're enough. They stiffen the hair on the back of my neck, send cold rivers of adrenalin down my arms, tighten my chest. They take me straight into my mother's desperation, my poor mom with my sister's scarf over her head, the scarf that was among the clothes in the paper bag from the coroner's office, the things she had been wearing when she died. I had wondered if it was what she used to hang herself until I saw the electrical cord listed on her death certificate.

Get me away from here, I'm dying. I'm dying. I'm dying.

The baby looks into my eyes with the wise, direct gaze he's had since he was born. "He was brought here to be a healer," a friend said shortly after his birth, and it feels true. It feels as if he is the reason for my painful separation and divorce, as if he came when he did to help me get through this monstrous grief, to ground me with a pure and simple love. I don't want him to feel that responsibility his whole life, to be his mother's healer, but for now, I'll take it. "You're so naive," the song warns me, and maybe I am. I always cry at endings. I cry at beginnings, too. I lift my shirt, and he latches on, and I am all tears and milk and sweet, deep ache, alive with the mothers I've lost.

role / model

MICHAEL AND I HAD LUNCH AT THE CASTLE TODAY, a new Middle Eastern restaurant in the unincorporated stretch between Riverside and San Bernardino. The lentil soup was fantastic, spiked with lemon. The Lebanese salad was tart and fresh, a dice of cucumber and tomato and mint. The place is new but also not. I can't remember if you and I ever went there together back when it was still Pitruzello's, back when you were still alive—I don't think so, even though I can picture you in one of the booths, your pale skin glowing against the black vinyl; I can picture you there the way you looked before I was born, when people mistook you for Audrey Hepburn, your hair in a short beehive, a cigarette between your fingers. I can't remember if I ever told you I answered the restaurant's call for lunchtime tearoom models when I was nineteen. Probably not. As much as you wanted your girls to be open with you, more often than not your measuring gaze shut us down.

I'm not sure what compelled me to respond to the ad they placed in the *San Bernardino Sun* almost three decades ago. I hated modeling as a kid—I was too shy, too self-conscious in front of the camera. I cried at almost every audition, every photo shoot. I didn't see myself as the modeling type at nineteen, either. I was a hippie chick with hairy armpits and legs, a sophomore in college. I had gained more than the freshman fifteen, eating three cafeteria meals a day, the only vegetarian options being cheesy, starchy casseroles like lasagna and enchiladas. My belly stuck out nearly as far as my small breasts; my face was almost as round as it had been when I was on long-term steroids a few years before. When I looked in the mirror, all I saw was awkwardness; all I saw were flaws. But I answered the ad, and it was probably because you had been a tearoom model as a young woman, wearing structured dresses with cinched belts that accentuated the twenty-three-inch waist you had been so proud of when you were a model, your "little pinched-in waist," you liked to call it. You walked around a special parlor at Blum's Vogue, displaying couture for women who could afford the personal shopping service; you used the posture you had learned at the Patricia Stevens Finishing School in downtown Chicago, where you strode across rooms with books stacked on your head.

One of the pictures on your composite from your youthful modeling days shows you in a frothy negligee, the hem floating upward as if you had just spun around, your mouth a surprised O, like a blow-up doll's. You were dating your sister's psychiatrist at the time, the married man you fell in love with when you were sixteen. Did you think of him when you were twirling for the photographer, the chiffon lifting from your thighs?

The day I last saw you alive brought home how much care you usually devoted to your appearance. You looked sweaty and disheveled, your face bare, and you smelled bad—not a trace of Joy, your signature fragrance, on your skin. That was deeply disconcerting, almost as disconcerting as the paranoia that gripped you. It was clear that this psychotic episode was different from all the others—before, even when you were delusional, you looked good, put together in your artsy, middle-aged–woman Chico's clothes. No one other than your family would know by looking at you that something was wrong. Now, anyone could glance at your eyes, your general deshabille, and tell you were disturbed.

I, on the other hand, look rumpled most of the time. You always wanted to brush my hair, to buy me more "professional" clothes.

You would always give me samples of Clinique makeup that piled, unused, in my bathroom drawer. You would make references to "when you start wearing makeup" as if it was inevitable, as if one day, I would embrace the womanly arts. It frustrated you that I considered beauty regimens a foreign language. You were never overtly critical of my appearance, but you would get your passive-aggressive digs in. Whenever you saw your daughters after a long stretch, you would ask me if I had gained weight, and Elizabeth if she had lost weight. It was a well-established beauty hierarchy in our family, at least, from my perspective. Elizabeth has been taller than I since she was twelve and I was sixteen; she is stylish and confident, a head-turner. I was stunned when I first met her husband and overheard him whisper, "I don't think she's prettier than you" into her ear. I had considered it a priori that she was the more beautiful sister, had never imagined she could have any doubts about this.

Elizabeth was much more successful during our short stint as child models; she was younger and cuter and didn't cry during auditions. She got amazing gigs: the *Star Wars* Play-Doh set box; the 1977 cover of *Volume Feeding Institutions Magazine*, where she's a pint-size, turtlenecked women's libber, holding a sign that says, "WOMAN'S WORK IS NEVER DONE."

My big break came when the Spiegel people called. Spiegel catalogs were my pornography—I drooled over the glossy pages of the thick book, stoking fevered fantasies of fiber-optic lamps and dolls that could eat and pee. My first published work—a letter to Santa in the local paper—was essentially a handwritten, slightly embellished, Spiegel catalog shopping list. You drove me to the photo shoot; you drove our whole foray into modeling. You wanted the world to see your girls. My yellow T-shirt and lime-green gauchos felt scratchy; the silky, faux-Hermès scarf you had knotted around my neck made me swallow funny. You had a thing about scarves even then, although you didn't wear them religiously, the way you did to hide your neck when you got older.

The Spiegel people had asked me to dress in yellow and green to match the Crayola logo, since I'd be demonstrating the company's "Home Art Studio." I felt good about that. Art was something I understood. I liked art. I might not even have to cry.

The first thing the photographers did, much to your disappointment, was to remove the scarf. "Too mature," they said. They tied bows of thick, green yarn around my ponytail holders. They led me and another girl to the set, a faux family room, complete with pale wood paneling and brown shag carpet. An easel was set up there. The one side facing the camera already had a painting pinned to it, obviously done by an adult who was trying to paint like a kid—a yellow house, a yellow sun, a few washes of blue for the sky, a tree. The grass was only partially painted in. "Linda" was written at the bottom, in large, studiously childish letters.

They handed me a paintbrush. "Pretend to paint the grass," they said. I started to sweep the brush across the paper as if I were in the midst of a creative frenzy.

"No!" they yelled. "Just hold it against the painting."

I held the paintbrush there for what felt like ages. My arm got more and more tired, and I got more and more pissed off. I was not Linda. This was not my painting. When we were done, the girl on the other side of the easel, the one who really got to use the chalkboard since it wasn't on camera, trotted up to the photographer and, coached by her mom, chirped. "When are you going to use me again?" You encouraged me to say something similar, but I couldn't even look at the photographer as we left the studio.

The lady on the phone told me to come to Pitruzello's with my face "done" and to bring two pairs of pumps, one white, one black; she also instructed me to wear "flesh-colored" pantyhose. I bought drugstore makeup, cheap vinyl Payless shoes; the only thing I didn't have to buy was the pantyhose. I rarely wore hose, but I had lots of it, in every color—from red fishnet to sparkly, sheer black—thanks to Pairtree, the briefly lived mail-order subscription pantyhose company you and Dad had started.

As soon as I walked into the restaurant in my Indian-print sundress and Birkenstocks, my pumps in a plastic bag, I felt flimsy and unprepared. It was a sprawling Italian place, very old-school, with those dark, shiny booths and little areas that looked like grottos, fake grapes and Chianti bottles dripping everywhere. Supposedly the Rat Pack and JFK had dined there in its heyday. My face itched from the makeup. Bits of hair stuck through the legs of my hose, and the dim lights brought out the other hair flattened underneath the nylon.

I was directed to a room off to the side of the restaurant, a room normally used for private banquets. The blond, tired-eyed woman in charge looked me up and down with a cool, appraising eye.

"Try this on," she said, holding out a little pastel blue sailor suit, like something a tap dancer or a toddler would wear. The top had a typical nautical bib; the bottom had flared short-shorts. I would never wear such a thing, but I took the hanger from her hand.

"Where do I change?" I asked her.

"Right here," she said, and I could feel my cheeks grow hot. I didn't like undressing in front of strangers. I didn't think to wear a bra. I didn't own a bra. I should have had the foresight to pick one up when I bought the other girlie accoutrements.

I turned my back to her as I tried on the outfit. It left a swath of my belly bare, which I hadn't anticipated, but otherwise fit perfectly.

The woman seemed to approve. "So, tell me about yourself," she said.

"I'm going to the University of Redlands," I told her, "studying poetry and dance."

"Dance," she said, tapping her lip. "Maybe I could use you in one of my fashion shows."

I felt flattered that she thought I was fashion-show material.

"What kind of dancing do you do?" she asked.

"Modern," I told her. "Mostly improvisational."

"Show me," she said.

And so I busted out some interpretative dance moves there in the back room of Pitruzello's, swooping around like Isadora Duncan in my white pleather pumps and little sailor suit. The woman flinched and shook her head.

"That's not going to work," she said, and I felt immediately embarrassed, wobbly in the unfamiliar heels.

The woman instructed me about my duties: I was to go from table to table and tell people about the outfit, especially how much it cost. Panic stabbed my gut. I had pictured walking around the room silently as I modeled the clothes. A synonym for model is "dummy," and I had counted upon this, had counted upon being voiceless, just a body moving through space. I was deeply shy; it didn't help that I was also self-conscious about my mouth. This was pre-orthodontia, so I still had protruding eye teeth and always smiled with my mouth closed. I didn't want to have to talk to anyone.

Thankfully it was early—the restaurant had just opened for lunch, and only two tables were filled in the cavernous place. This was the training hour—the established models would arrive for the lunch rush. The woman led me to the first table, where a businessman and woman sat waiting for their meal. I stood in front of them, unsure what to say. The blond woman gave me a little nudge.

"Hi," I said, as brightly as I could. My voice didn't sound like itself. "I'd like to show you this adorable sailor suit, if you don't mind."

"Go right on ahead, darling," the man said, looking amused. He was probably in his forties, wearing a suit.

I babbled something about the clothes being machine-washable and great for a day at the beach and only $29.99. I felt as if I were going to throw up.

"Can you spin around?" the man asked. I glanced as his lunch companion—was she his coworker? Girlfriend? Wife? She looked down at the empty plate before her.

I turned haltingly, feeling his eyes travel over my body. I felt uncomfortable but also flattered. I looked young for my age and wasn't used to that kind of male attention, other than from my boyfriend. A couple of poet boys had crushes on me, but they gazed at me as if I were a fairy princess, not as if they wanted to rip my clothes off.

"Very nice," he said. "Turn around again, slower this time." I glanced over at my supervisor; she gave a subtle nod, so I did another twirl, taking even more time, like a music-box dancer winding down.

When I thanked the man, he winked at me and said, "No, thank *you*" in the most lascivious way; his lunch companion glanced at me and briefly smiled, perhaps in pity, before her eyes flicked away again.

My supervisor led me to the other table. I was relieved when the two women in the booth said, "No, thanks," and turned to their menus as soon as I started my pitch.

"Not bad for your first time," the woman said as we walked back to the banquet room. This time, she gave me my pick of outfits. I can't say why I went for the sheer, black negligee. I had never worn lingerie before. There were other outfits laid out on the long banquet table—halter-top dresses, A-line skirts—but for some reason, I chose the teddy. Was it for the man who had asked me to spin around? Was it to satisfy my own curiosity? Was I thinking about the lingerie shot on your composite, Mom? I honestly have no clue—I didn't then, either. I just plucked it from the table, and the woman said, "You're really going for it, aren't you?"

"I guess so," I said.

"You're going to have to shave your pits next time," she told me and handed me two round Band-Aids to cover my nipples.

I walked straight over to the table with the man and the woman in my little nightie and my black pumps. The Band-Aids were clear as day through the barely there fabric. The v of the neckline plunged below my breastbone. I held my upper arms close to the side of my body so my armpit hair wouldn't show.

Before I could say anything about the outfit, the man reached out and touched my hip, where the little skirt flared.

"You look good," he said. "You look *really* good." He didn't move his hand, let it settle more firmly. I could feel the heat of it travel through my hose, his thick fingertips pressing deep.

His lunch had arrived. Shrimp scampi. The tangle of shrimp, glistening with butter, looked obscene, like an orgy in the shallow bowl. I started to feel dizzy. When I looked away, I noticed all the statues of naked men that ringed the courtyard just outside the dining room, dozens of Davids in concrete; dozens of penises crowding me in. The man's hand curved around to cup my ass. I looked to my supervisor, but she didn't breathe a word. She just looked at me as if to say, "Say something"—something about the outfit, not something about this strange man with his hand on my body. My voice stuck in my throat.

"It's only $19.99," I managed to stammer before I walked back to the banquet room and changed into my own clothes.

"I don't think this is for me," I told the woman, my whole body trembling.

"Call me if you change your mind," she said. The other models were starting to arrive. They seemed friendly enough. Much taller and thinner and more polished than I, more like the models you would see in catalogs. I felt like a potato next to them, short and shapeless. I left so quickly, I forgot to grab my new pairs of pumps.

Many years later, I learned that one of my best friends had been a tearoom model in the 1960s. One day, while she was modeling a little tennis outfit, a man grabbed her ass, and she swatted him with her tennis racket. I wish I had been able to have struck back in such a firm, clear way, but I didn't have it in me. Another definition of "model" is "a figure or object made in clay or wax, to be reproduced in another, more durable material." I was still made of clay, of wax, malleable stuff. I was just learning how to use my body, and outside of poetry, I had no idea how to use my voice. There was so much I had to learn, so much I didn't know. And who am I kidding? There's still so much I have to learn, so very much I still don't know.

I don't know how you knew how to hang yourself, Mom, how to wrap that random electrical cord around your neck in a way that would work. You didn't learn it in finishing school; they didn't teach girls how to finish themselves in that way. But the surveillance camera showed you walking upright, regal, into the small room in the parking garage where you ended your life, walking as if you had a stack of books on your head.

Your death fucked me up. More than I let myself realize at the time. After you died, I tried to put all my focus on my new baby, on the joy he brought, but your death lived inside me, a constant companion I tried to ignore. Then Michael's mom died from a sudden heart attack less than four months later, and that fucked us both up, individually and as a couple. We didn't realize how much it had fucked us up because we each kept it to ourselves, kept it hidden from ourselves. It got to the point where we could barely look at one another, we were both seething with so much unspoken, unacknowledged resentment. All we could see was our own bitterness projected onto one another's face.

I suppose it's not surprising that I fell in love with a man who called me beautiful, a man who seemed to fully see and appreciate me as both a woman and writer. He was the kind of man you had envisioned for me, Mom——worldly, talented, a best-selling author; he was closer to your age than mine, and I know you would have found him as charming as I did; you would have flirted outrageously with him; you would have put yourself, as you often did, in competition with your daughter. He lived on the other side of the country, so we communicated by email, and eventually by Skype. He joked that he wanted to see me in a wet T-shirt, so one day when Asher was in preschool, I wore a T-shirt into the shower. I felt sexy there, the hot water plastering the cotton to my skin. I felt sexy as I took a picture of myself, drenched and full of longing. It was the first modeling assignment I had ever enjoyed, the first time I could remember feeling completely comfortable in front of a camera. I sent it to him with the subject line, "Ask and ye shall receive."

It quickly became a compulsion, taking and sending photos of myself to this man, and eventually, he asked me to stop. "This isn't helping either one of us," he wrote, but that wasn't true. Yes, it was frustrating that we were thousands of miles away from one another, that I was married, that we couldn't do anything about our attraction; yes, it was stressful to vigilantly erase all the photos and messages from my phone; yes, I felt guilty, but it *was* helping me, immeasurably. At forty-five, it was helping me see myself as beautiful, unabashedly beautiful, for maybe the first time in my life. It was helping me see myself as someone worthy of desire, someone worthy of the lens. Something I hadn't even known I had wanted.

Michael and I separated in the midst of my obsession, and I finally rendezvoused with the man I had fallen for. I let my expectations billow, let my heart get soundly broken. Michael and I reconciled a few months later; I'm grateful he's been so patient and forgiving, although my lapse continues to haunt us. Michael often tells me how beautiful he finds me now, how much he desires me, and while I love to hear this and know his words are sincere, I don't feel beautiful the way I did for a stretch of time last year; I no longer see myself through that same incandescent lens. Now if I take pictures of myself, the thing I see most often is you, Mom. That self-conscious, hopeful look you would get when you had your picture taken. Your hope that the camera would capture the

woman you wanted to be; your hope that your best, most glorious
self would shine through, that the perfect paragon (another synonym for "model") of Arlene June Baylen Brandeis would finally
show herself; your self-consciousness making it impossible for the
ideal you to fully come to the surface. It makes me sad that I can
see this in my own face now.

The owners of The Castle have kept most of Pitruzello's
decor—all the great, old shiny booths are still there—but they've
neutered the David statues, lopped their penises right off, leaving
crumbling swaths of concrete between their legs. As uncomfortable
as those penises once made me, seeing them destroyed disturbed
me even more. Desire is dangerous—I get that now, I get that
fully—but we can't pretend it doesn't exist. We have to learn how
to live with these messy, pining bodies of ours. I thought maybe
the new owners were religious, averse to overt displays of flesh, but
they seem to have no problem with the female body; the restaurant
features belly dancers a few nights a week. I may, in fact, become
one of those dancers—my friend who invited me to be part of
her troupe has approached the owners about performing there.
Wouldn't that be wild if I were to dance in that space, belly bare
again decades after I'd donned that little sailor suit? I would be
much more comfortable moving between the tables now; I'm never
more at home in my skin than when I dance.

Still, I can't stop seeing the ghost of my younger self walking
around the restaurant in that black nightie and cheap pumps,
Band-Aids on her nipples, head jutting forward, uncertain about
every step. So much of that girl is still in me. That girl is trying
to be you and trying not to be you in equal measure. That girl
never went to finishing school. That girl will never be finished.
That girl still feels awkward much of the time, is still unsure how
to be a woman in the world. That girl doesn't know how to be
your daughter, especially now that you're gone. She can't save
you anymore; she knows now she never could. All she can do is

unwrap the scarf from her own throat, the scarf you had knotted there so she could become Linda for the Spiegel catalog people, a name she later learned means "beautiful." Linda has had more of a hold on the girl than she had realized.

The girl looks in the mirror at her bare neck. It is not a girl's neck anymore; it is a middle-aged woman's neck now, starting to crepe and droop—it is the part of her body that shows her age the most; that and her hands, which now look like yours, topped with ropy blue veins. The girl tries not to cringe; she forces herself to look past the loose skin and see the pulse, the lifeblood ticking there. The pulse you wrenched silent in your own neck, your neck whose looseness caused you so much angst. The girl doesn't want to inherit your angst. She doesn't want to care whether other people find her beautiful. She takes a deep breath, feels the air whoosh into her body. She wants to keep her throat wide open; she wants to use her throat to live.

joy

"Scent of the century"

—*Fragrance Foundation FiFi Awards, 2000*

THE PERFUME IS CALLED JOY, BUT THE BLACK BOX looked sinister to me as a kid, funereal; it looked as if it should hold ashes, cigarettes, a lifeless heart. The perfume didn't smell joyful to me, either—it smelled like sugar laced with poison. I couldn't understand why my mother loved it so, why my father bought it for her so religiously—tiny bottles in a cushioned box, a larger bottle for extra-special occasions. I was told it was expensive, rare, told it was the most generous gift, but it bothered me, felt like something between my parents I couldn't access, some terrifying adult brand of joy.

∽

Jean Patou journeyed to the South of France in 1926 to find a perfume that could recharge his haute couture business, hammered by the Great Depression. He didn't like any of the samples Henri Alméras offered up, until the famous perfumer produced the yet-unnamed Joy. "If you don't like this," he said, "I'll get a job herding goats."

∽

The perfume smelled better on my mom; mixed with the heat of her body, it smelled less caustic, more like her, but even then, it made me shudder, made me feel a bit sick. She wore it when she went on dates with my dad, when my sister and I would weepingly chase them down the hall of our building, pressing the elevator button so the door would open again, and they weren't able to leave; we did this until the babysitter pulled us back to our apartment, where the Joy was still so heavy in the air, it closed my throat.

Patou loved the yet-unnamed Joy, but Alméras warned him it would be wildly expensive to produce. Patou's confidante, society columnist Elise Maxwell, perked up and said that could be their whole shtick. They'd market it as the costliest perfume in the world.

When I was nine or ten, I formed a girl out of green clay, those little cylinders that come stuck together in a pack, and smell of glue and soil. I shaped a dress with a collar, shaped two little feet with shoelaces, hair that curled into a flip. I had never sculpted anything so lifelike before. I was proud of it and stuck it inside one of the gold boxes that had held Joy—so much better than the black Joy boxes, a J and P curled into a kind of yin-yang on the top, a box that snapped open like a book—for safekeeping. I didn't realize I had created a golem of sorts, the word "Joy" imprinted on her forehead by the phantom scent of the perfume, the word "Joy" slipping inside the girl's closed mouth, beneath her invisible tongue.

Each ounce of Joy, it is said, contains 10,600 jasmine flowers, and twenty-eight dozen roses—the Damascene rose from Bulgaria, the Rose de Mai and Jasminum grandiflorum from Grasse in the South of France. Joy smelled chemical to me, something made in a science lab; I was surprised to learn it was made of real flowers, whole fields crushed into gold.

⁂

I've never been a perfume person—it tends to make my eyes water, constrict my breath—but I did dabble a bit when I was young. I still remember how a sample vial of "Rain"—a natural perfume, perhaps a mix of essential oils—smelled at a shop near my junior high, which sold locally handmade goods; I never purchased it but twisted the little brown bottle open whenever I visited the store with my friends. They would smell each vial in the row of artisanal perfumes, and I'd stick to Rain, would inhale it until its scent filled my whole body, would put a dab behind my ears, rub some between my inner wrists the way I'd heard you're supposed to do—something about the skin being thinner there, more porous. The slick of fragrance didn't smell like petrichor, one of my favorite scents, but it did have an essential raininess to it, deep and sweet and wet. I loved walking into the world with it on my skin, though not enough to ever purchase it. I didn't feel ready to own the scent somehow; it was enough to play at the thought of being a girl who wore perfume, to pretend to be a girl who smelled like Rain.

⁂

Of course, it didn't make sense to sell an expensive perfume during the Depression, but Patou found a way to make it work. He sent free bottles of Joy to two hundred fifty prominent American women in 1930, telling them, "If you can't afford our couture, we know you'll still want something desirable." Perfume as a dose of luxury during lean times. This was nine years before my mother was born, but she must have absorbed the message somehow. She grew up in a blue-collar household and longed for a life of glamour. My dad was able to give her a taste of the world she wanted, bringing her to nice restaurants, to the theater, to the opera, but it was never enough. She wanted to buy houses we couldn't afford, wanted to shop at Saks Fifth Avenue even after my dad's direct mail marketing company went bankrupt. When her delusional disorder surfaced, it seemed fitting that her delusions were centered around money, that she believed my dad was hiding millions of dollars from her, money that could have kept her swimming in Joy.

I associate Joy exclusively with my mom, but, of course, she wasn't the only person to wear it. Marilyn Monroe, Vivien Leigh, Josephine Baker, Jackie Kennedy, Wallis Simpson, Gloria Swanson, Queen Elizabeth, Audrey Hepburn, and other celebrities favored the scent. Keith Richards reportedly has used it as deodorant. I imagine my mom felt like a celebrity, felt like royalty when she wore it, swathed in rarefied air.

The first perfume I ever bought (and, now that I think about it, only perfume I'd ever bought until just recently)—was the ubiquitous Love's Baby Soft when I was twelve or thirteen. All the girls I knew reeked of it, as did the girls' locker room at school. Love's Baby Soft came in what looked like a bottle of pink juice with a rounded pink plastic top and had a cotton candy–like scent. The slogan plastered on its ads in the pages of *Tigerbeat* and *Seventeen*— "Because innocence is sexier than you think"—was (horrifyingly) accompanied by a glamour shot of a girl who appeared to be about nine years old, clutching a teddy bear, lipstick on her pouty mouth, hair coiffed in a pageant do. I worried about this girl whenever I saw this ad, worried about who considered her sexy, about what that person must have done to her. Her face looked vacant, haunted. I was curious to know what sexiness would feel like inside myself, wanted to carry it under my girl skin like a secret fragrance only I could smell.

⋈

Joy is not just made of roses and jasmine from Grasse. According to parfumo.com, it has top notes of aldehyde, green notes, peach, rose, tuberose, and ylang-ylang, heart notes of orris root, jasmine, lily of the valley, orchid, and rose; and base notes of musk, sandalwood, and civet. I hadn't realized perfumes have top, heart, and base notes; I envy those who can detect them, just as I envy those who can detect all the different notes of wine.

⋈

I was surprised to learn that Love's Baby Soft shares rose and jasmine heart notes with Joy though certainly not the same quantity or quality of those blossoms (if Love's Baby Soft even uses real blossoms). It also holds lily of the valley at its heart, with top notes of lemon leaf and orange, and base notes of sandalwood, vanilla, "powdery notes," and musk. Apparently, the perfume is supposed to smell like clean babies—that was the perfume's whole, creepy seventies deal, making girls and women smell like clean, sexy babies. Powder and musk.

⋈

I did like the smell of Joy body powder, liked the big, soft powder puff inside the round, black box that sat on the tank of my parents' toilet—that powder smelled like pulverized SweeTARTS to me, SweeTARTS and the Scratch and sniff flowers from Pat the Bunny. Joy for Kids.

⸙

In *Perfume: An A-Z Guide*, Luca Turin writes, "To call Joy a floral is to misunderstand it, since the whole point of its formula... was to achieve the platonic ideal of a flower, not one earthly manifestation."

⸙

Maybe the golden box that holds the green girl, the golem, is a cryogenic chamber of sorts, keeping my childhood alive there, intact. Platonic.

⸙

About a year ago, I happened upon a magazine ad for Joy: Jennifer Lawrence in a swimming pool up to her neck, not looking very joyful. In fact, her face looked more like the sexy little girl in the Love's Baby Soft ad, slightly vacant and haunted, her lips parted in a way that was clearly supposed to be sexy but struck me more as incomprehension. The cylindrical bottle of Joy in the corner of the ad didn't look like the Joy I knew—it looked more like Love's Baby Soft, in fact, the perfume pink, not the gold my mother loved. "Dior" was written in the middle of the O of JOY, which surprised me—could two companies have a perfume by the same name? I did a quick search and learned that Jean Patou's company had gone through a few different owners—it was purchased by Procter

& Gamble in 2001, then by Designer Parfums in 2011, and by LVMH in 2018. LVMH, which also owns Dior, released the new Joy, with a new scent, under that label the same year.

When I was a freshman in high school, I participated in a service club that sent busloads of mostly white students from our North Shore suburbs to tutor kids at a community center in a Latinx neighborhood of Chicago every weekend. I became friendly with the eight-year-old boy I tutored, and—even though this was likely not something my school would have endorsed—invited him to my house. When we picked him up, he was wearing a button-down shirt and had his hair slicked back, as if he was going someplace fancy, not our aluminum-sided house, where we would slide down the carpeted basement steps together on a foam chair that unfolded into a small bed, over and over again, screaming with laughter. His mother, who didn't speak English, smiled and handed me a wrapped box containing an Avon gift set of jasmine-scented perfume, lotion, and powder. It felt romantic, somehow, as if I were going on a date with both her and her dressed-up eight-year-old son. The jasmine set sat untouched in my bathroom cabinet for months, until I started having periods and used the jasmine perfume to mask the scent of the blood on the pads I made out of wads of folded, yellow Kleenex. I didn't tell my mother about my periods for a year; I didn't want my parents to know I was growing up, wanted to stay the green girl in the golden box forever.

In a press release, Dior perfumer François Demachy said, "JOY by Dior expresses this remarkable feeling of joy by offering an olfactive interpretation of light. This perfume resembles certain pointillist paintings that are rich with a precise, yet not too obvious, technique. It is constructed with multiple nuances, a myriad of facets that lead to an expression that is clear and self-evident." Most reviews were not nearly so rhapsodic nor cryptic, saying the perfume was nice but paled in comparison to the iconic Patou original. The blog Colognoisseur notes, "Joy by Dior is a good perfume put together via the perfume assembly line of focus groups and market research; as cynical as it gets, in other words."

Cynicism: the anthesis of joy.

Merriam-Webster defines joy as:

1. a : the emotion evoked by well-being, success, or good fortune or by the prospect of possessing what one desires : DELIGHT

   b : the expression or exhibition of such emotion : GAIETY
2. a state of happiness or felicity : BLISS
3. a source or cause of delight

I keep looking at the end of 1 a, "the prospect of possessing what one desires." Is the desire for something more joyful than the possession of that thing? Did my mom find more joy in anticipating the gift of Joy than she did in the Joy itself?

There is one moment in the Joy TV commercial with Jennifer Lawrence—a commercial otherwise filled with standard, woman-swimming-in-a–ball gown perfume ad fare—that feels like real, not consumer-driven, joy, a moment where she spits a stream of pool water out of her mouth and bursts into laughter. Joy as silliness, as wildness, as DELIGHT, GAIETY, BLISS.

If I were to make my own blend of joyful scents, it would include
the burnt-sugar toastiness of the top of my newborns' heads; the
mustiness of old books; the chlorine/fish-food tang of Chicago's
Shedd Aquarium; the gasolined air of my childhood apartment's
garage; the orange blossom–thick air near the experimental groves
at UC Riverside; the sweetness of my mother's poppyseed cake in
the oven (her noodle kugel, too); the mineral scent of stones wet
with lake water; the chilled rubber of my childhood ice rink's floor;
the beer-soaked, incense-tinged, hallway of my college dorm; the
clean warmth of my kids fresh from a bath; the spiced comfort of
my husband's chest; the sweet funk of a room after sex. I'd toss in
other scents I love—some sagebrush, some ginger, some honeydew
and rose water, the richness of my own blood unmasked. I'd toss
in both Rain and rain.

My mom didn't learn to swim until she was forty, but she became
an avid swimmer from that point forward. If she went a day
without swimming, she felt off, didn't feel like herself. She would
have enjoyed seeing Jennifer Lawrence in that pool—she liked
perfume ads with pools, told me when I was twelve that in a
commercial for Chanel No. 5, the shadow of a plane flying over
a swimming pool was a metaphor for sex, which made me want
to run away screaming. Still, I think she would have scoffed at
the new Joy. She'd have said it doesn't have the elegance of the
original. Elegance was important to her. She'd have said the new
perfume looks like it's for a little girl, would have fixed me with
a hard stare.

✻

Maybe the green girl in the golden box is my stunted self. Maybe that golem held onto me with her damp clay arms and kept me from fully growing up.

✻

The new version of Joy has silver thread wrapped around its cap; the iconic 1930 Joy bottle, designed by architect Louis Süe, had golden thread around its neck. I had forgotten this detail, and when I saw the phrase "golden thread around its neck" as I researched the perfume, I shuddered. Did my mom ever see the thread around the neck of Joy and know that's how her own life would end?

✻

I ordered samples of the Patou Joy and the Dior Joy (the above-mentioned, post–Love's Baby Soft perfume purchase) from a company that sells samples of various sizes, decanted from larger bottles. I ordered the site's smallest samples—one milliliter each. I knew I couldn't handle more than that, knew I just wanted a whiff of each one. The Patou sample was $4.96, the Dior $3.49. The tiny vials arrived wrapped in a sheet of foam inside a silver net bag, along with a single espresso candy. Grown-up candy.

✻

Maybe the green girl in the golden box is now the girl inside me, who keeps returning to her mother's death, the girl who thought she was done writing about her mother's death, who thought this would be a piece about scent, not grief, but how could it not be about grief, the way scent is so evanescent, so connected with memory, so connected with her mother's vanished body?

I was scared to open the vials of scent. I didn't feel ready to smell my mom again, even though I was eager to get the last whiff I'd had of her—the stench of her death on the clothing we received in a paper bag from the coroner's office—out of my brain. Maybe the perfume would knock that scent memory away. I could easily conjure up the smell of Joy, but the thought of actually having it in my nose again felt terrifying.

Jean Patou said, "Just like men, perfume is never perfect right away; you have to let it seduce you," but I don't think a perfume could ever seduce me, even though other scents can. When we were falling in love, I craved the scent of my husband's natural musk, needed it like food, loved to smell it on my skin hours after his skin had touched mine. I still love, still need that scent.

I opened the Dior Joy first, since I don't have any emotion, any memory connected with it. I tried to smell it once, with my sister, in the midst of a family reunion in Chicago to celebrate what would have been our dad's hundredth birthday. We went to Marshall Field's, department store of our childhood, and I pointed out a gift set of Dior's Joy on a shelf. We opened the white box, curious to know what this new Joy smelled like, but the box was empty.

Maybe the green girl in the golden box wasn't afraid to grow up. Maybe she was just afraid to grow up and become her mother. Maybe that girl didn't know there were other ways of being a woman in the world. Maybe it took her a while to learn this. Maybe it took her a while to figure out someday she'd be happy to be an adult, happy to recognize certain aspects of her mother inside her.

The stopper of the tiny vial was attached to a plastic stem that dipped into the perfume, like a slender bubble wand. I tipped my nose closer and almost instantly regretted it. There's a reason I've been staying away from perfume—I'm not just averse to it, I'm allergic. Mildly compared to some but enough to make me uncomfortable. I didn't think to arm myself with antihistamines beforehand; what damage could one little sniff do? My throat immediately narrowed; my eyes started to burn. The perfume reminded me more of Love's Baby Soft than Patou's Joy but with a more grown-up bite. I couldn't tell you the base notes, heart notes, or top notes, but I can say it transported me to my aunt's perfumed bathroom, to childhood trips to the theater, engulfed in clashing layers of scent. I ripped open the espresso candy and popped it into my mouth, as if it could be a palate cleanser, could suck the fragrance from my nose, but, of course, that didn't help. Even when I opened our sliding glass door, the scent remained.

The tagline in the original French ads for Joy was "le parfum le plus cher du monde"; not the most expensive perfume in the world—the most beloved.

I still haven't opened the vial of Patou's Joy. I haven't felt ready to let that genie out of the bottle, haven't felt ready for the scent to linger in the air after I've had enough. Now it sits in my house like a telltale heart, like a cyanide pill, like a time capsule I'm nervous to open, maybe a time machine that could disrupt the world.

∞

Maybe the green girl in the golden box is a golem of the little girl who would press the elevator button over and over as her parents tried to leave, Joy heavy in the air, wailing, *Don't Go Don't Go Don't Go Don't Go.*

sugar in the blood

S UGAR FILLS MY FAMILY'S BLOOD.
    My mother had diabetes; many of her nine siblings had diabetes; both her parents had diabetes; her father had both legs amputated because of diabetes; one of my cousins died young from diabetes (and before that, her fetus died within her from diabetes). 23andMe tells me I have a higher-than-average likelihood of developing diabetes, to which I say, "Ya think?" The sap in our family tree doesn't need to be boiled down for syrup—it already runs thick with treacle.

Diabetes mellitus literally means "honeyed siphon," a misleadingly beautiful name, one that sounds like being deep in creative flow. I love when I feel like a honeyed siphon, a vessel words pour through, all lubed up with sweet inspiration. The honeyed siphon of diabetes, of course, is not nearly so lovely, glucose building in the blood, jacking up the kidneys and other organs, getting pissed out in such great quantities, a diabetic's urine turns to sugar crystals if left in the sun.

I had thought only my mother's side of the family tree was riddled with sweet blood. Then I found two articles about a paternal great grandfather, Joseph Sirasky—my father's mother's father—who had thrown himself from a third-floor window of Sinai Hospital in Baltimore the day before he was scheduled to have a diabetic leg amputated. He had asked a nurse to give him some time alone; a few minutes later, his body was found, skull fractured on the pavement.

I had thought only my mother's side of the tree was marked by suicide.

On 23andMe, I learn that some of my genetic relatives have common relatives on both sides of the family, the two halves apparently crossing somewhere near Kyiv long before my parents met in 1960s Chicago, our trunk braided like malabar chestnuts. Perhaps a pull toward oblivion runs through our whole tree, our sap sludgy with it, as well as all that stubborn sugar. Perhaps both are time bombs in my blood. Will I recognize if one detonates within me? Will I be able to name the explosion, or will I get caught in its shock wave, tumbling through its current like any other corpuscle? Does the desire to leave this world feel like its own kind of honeyed siphon, a sweet slide into the void?

(I should say the only time the words "I want to die" roared into my head did not feel sweet. It felt like fire, like smoke, like choking. This was during the Caldor Fire; our world was burning, the flames headed in our direction, the sky so smoky, I could barely breathe, even with the windows closed, the air purifiers running. It felt as if the earth were dying, and I wanted to die with her, didn't want to live in a world where my beloved trees were burned to a crisp, the bears and ravens turned to ash.)

Perhaps the time bomb of diabetes set off the time bomb of suicide within my mother. She treated her diabetes with diet and exercise, and likely should have been doing more. Most of the time, she had the condition under control, but her blood sugar spiked the month before her death. Once, when I showed up at her house, she could barely speak, just held up her glucose monitor, a ridiculously high digital number blinking, a bead of blood still on her punctured fingertip. High blood sugar can lead to mood changes, to anxiety, even to hallucinations. I don't think diabetes caused the delusional disorder that plagued the last two decades of my mother's life, but perhaps it exacerbated some of her psychotic episodes. I tried to convince her to let me bring her to the ER, but she didn't want to go. "If it takes me, it takes me," she said, reminding me that she had a "Do not resuscitate" order, words she planned to have tattooed upon her chest.

Before the role of insulin was discovered in 1910, treatments around the world for diabetes included horseback riding, starvation diets, overfeeding to compensate for dehydration, wine. The book *Ashkenazi Herbalism* tells me my ancestors likely used clover to treat diabetes, and sometimes raspberry, fruit that looks like globs of sweet blood, but pre-insulin, diabetes was often a death sentence. Sometimes, of course, it still is.

(We decided to leave the area, the Caldor smoke too much to bear, and I couldn't help but think of my ancestors who likely had to flee fire as Cossacks charged through their villages on horseback, torching their homes. On each step of our small exodus—so much smaller than my ancestors' flight to safety—I couldn't help but imagine our home, the woods around it, aflame. I imagined this so much that when we finally returned, I was shocked to find our neighborhood uncharred, shocked to find it green, even, wild strawberry leaves still tender across the forest floor. Strawberries were used in Ashkenazi herbalism, too; my ancestors likely made infusions of the dried leaves and berries for pain in the chest, for cough and other maladies. I hope they found wild strawberries in the midst of their escape, found bits of forest sweetness as they moved toward the future that led to my parents, that led to me and my siblings and our children and all the generations yet to come, some with sugar in the blood, some not. I saw the strawberry leaves tender across the forest floor, and I wanted to live.)

My doctor tests my blood regularly for sugar. I try to test myself regularly for destructive impulses, try to test myself regularly to make sure I'm not sugarcoating anger or pain or grief, as has been my default, another kind of inherited sweetness, the toxic kind that pretends everything is okay, like the pink packets of saccharin my mother dumped into mugs of Taster's Choice, Sweet'n Low (where the patriarchy wants to keep us).

May our throats, our hands, our bodies be siphons that pump out the real stuff, honeyed only when honey is called for. May we resist the impulse to burn ourselves down.

IV

TACHYPNEA:

increased breathing rate

ghosts in the ecotone

WHEN YOU TAKE THE US 50 DOWN THE MOUNTAIN from Lake Tahoe to Carson City, Nevada, the landscape slowly shifts—the abundant pine trees start to thin, start to coexist with scrubbier desert plants. This is the ecotone, the liminal space where two landscapes bleed into one another. The trees continue to fade toward the bottom of the hill; one final pine stands sentinel on a granite outcropping before the ground flattens and sagebrush takes over.

We had recently moved from Southern California to North Lake Tahoe, and my whole body felt like an ecotone, full of shifting landscape. I watched the lone pine fade from view in the passenger-side mirror as my husband drove toward Virginia City, a historic mining town about an hour from our new home. I had been invited to a weekend retreat there and was excited to connect with other women writers from the area.

The timing was perfect. I'd been making good headway on my memoir about my mom, but between the move and settling into my new position as visiting professor, I wasn't finding much time for my own work. I planned to write like a hurricane at the retreat, but I also gave myself a personal challenge: to watch the documentary my mom had been wrapping up at the time of her death. I had stolen the title for my memoir, *The Art of Misdiagnosis*, from her film but hadn't viewed the movie since she hanged herself. At first, I hadn't felt ready, and then, once I started to entertain the idea, hadn't found the right span of time; now a whole weekend stretched before me, the DVD tucked in my backpack.

The landscape changed again. A twisty road took us from level desert into a canyon flanked by hills stripped of their ore, half their bulk sheared away. As we neared Virginia City, each sign by the roadside felt oracular, pointing toward my mom's story: SEE THE FAMOUS SUICIDE TABLE; LYNCH HOUSE; GOLD this and GOLD that. I can't see the word "gold" without thinking of my mom, her frantic search for the fortune she thought my dad was hiding from the family; my mom, who took the Gold Line from Union Station in L.A. to a random stop in South Pasadena, who somehow made her way to the parking garage of the Golden Oaks apartment complex, who lynched herself there. Gold upon gold upon gold.

We cruised past buildings from the mid-1800s—saloons and candy emporiums and souvenir shops—then turned onto a street that led downhill to an imposing four-story brick building with a broad, white-pillared veranda. Wild horses grazed on the front lawn; they barely looked up when we got out of the car.

Saint Mary's Art and Retreat Center is supposed to be one of the most haunted sites in America. Originally built in 1873 as a hospital for miners, it became a community hospital and asylum that closed in the 1940s, when the town's population dwindled. It has been an arts center since 1964. People still report hearing the rumble of carts and gurneys in the hall, smelling rubbing alcohol, seeing shadowy figures and bright orbs of light; people have noticed rumpled sheets after making the bed, fresh batteries running quickly out of juice. A "white nun" supposedly appears on a regular basis; many think she was the nurse who burned to death after a psychiatric patient knocked over a lamp. The building has been featured on television shows like *Ghost Hunters* and *Ghost Adventures* and is visited often by amateur paranormal investigators armed with electromagnetic field detectors and full-spectrum cameras and Michael the Archangel scapulars. Before he dropped me off, my own Michael joked that he and our son would come back at night and make scary noises outside my window.

I don't believe in the afterlife, yet I'm convinced my mom's ghost visited me about a week after she died. I was lying on my side in bed, nursing Asher, when I felt a hand on my shoulder. A strong, reassuring pressure. I knew it was my mom, that she had come to comfort me, to ask for my forgiveness, but I wasn't ready. I shrugged my shoulder, shrugged her away. I felt awful afterward, wanted to summon her back, wanted to feel her hand on my shoulder again, but she never returned.

The veil between what was real and what was not thinned during those postpartum days, those sleep-deprived, grief and hormone–soaked nights. Once, I woke Michael at three in the morning and told him, "My nipples are cracked, my breasts are full and they're on speaker phone." I told him the contestants had gone seven rounds already, and Asher hadn't had his turn. I knew I wasn't making sense, but somehow it was all clear in my head. I wondered if this was how my mom felt, trying to get us to understand that she was being followed and poisoned, trying to assure us her delusions were real.

Every time the door to my room rattled at Saint Mary's, I wondered if a ghost wanted in. Every time I felt a coolness on my neck, I wondered if a wraith had brushed against me. I saw no orbs, though, heard no moans; my sheets were rumpled but only because I chose to do my work on the iron-framed bed.

Shortly after I settled into my Victoriana-filled room, I decided not to put off the inevitable: I opened the plastic case with my mom's picture on the cover, clicked the DVD into Asher's portable player, popped Michael's buds into my ears. I took a deep breath as the disc started to whir. White words scrolled down the small screen, my mom's mission for the documentary: "I would like to save others from the pain, loss, and frustration my family has endured…" There was no sound; I worried the audio wasn't working and turned the volume all the way up. Soon, piano chords blasted my eardrums, and then my mom's disembodied voice, the first time I had heard it since her death: "I fully feel that the spirits of my family have propelled me to do this documentary." A sob ballooned in my chest, but I held it in and heaved quietly, not wanting to startle the women writing in the quiet rooms around me. When my mom's image appeared on the screen, my eyes were so full, I saw her through water—my mom, wavery and spectral as any ghost. My mom, once I blinked, alive and standing. My mom, speaking about illness as I sat in an old hospital. My mom, whose mental illness was never diagnosed, visiting me in an asylum.

My mom served as a docent at the Museum of Contemporary Art in Chicago and various museums in California and envisioned her film as a personal art tour exploring her own abstract art, paintings that addressed the illnesses she thought plagued her family. She wanted the film to draw attention to two rare diseases she felt were often mis- and underdiagnosed: porphyria, a metabolic disorder that can cause a range of symptoms, from stomach pain to werewolfism; and Ehlers-Danlos syndrome, a connective tissue disorder that can affect many systems of the body, primarily the skin, joints, and blood vessels. My mom, who was certain Ehlers-Danlos had led to her brothers' fatal heart attacks, fully expected her film to change the health care industry.

My sister and I had asked her not to talk about our own journeys with illness in the film, and we were majorly pissed off when she showed us the rough cut, where she talked at length about how she had saved her poor daughters from the dastardly medical establishment. She didn't talk about how both of us had malingered, how I had pretended to be ill long after I went into remission, how we had fabricated illness to further our identities as sick girls, to help her maintain her identity as mother of the sick girls. She didn't talk about it because she hadn't been able to hear us when we tried to tell her the truth; she was only able to hear her own story.

As I watched the documentary at Saint Mary's, I could feel myself getting pissed at her all over again, and I felt guilty for feeling angry at my dead mom. I wanted to come at her story from a place of compassion but found that anger kept bubbling up to the surface. I hoped I could write my way toward a more open heart.

And something in me must have opened that afternoon, at least a small crack, because just as my mom had felt the spirits of her family propel her to paint, propel her to make the documentary, I felt her spirit—freed genielike from a flat, silver disc—propel me to transcribe the film, to weave it into the book, to let her speak for herself.

When it was time to head downstairs to meet the other women for cocktail hour, I was shaky and raw, my mom's voice vibrating in my bones, her image burned into my retina. As we sat around the kitchen table covered with caprese salad and hummus and many bottles of wine, and the women each introduced themselves and their writing projects, I found myself choking back tears. *Hold it together*, I told myself, *don't be a wreck*, but when my turn came around, I blurted out, "I've been trying not to cry, but I'm just going to go ahead and let myself."

"Let it out, baby," a woman encouraged from across the table, and I did, I shared how wobbly I felt after sitting with my mom's moving image, and I was embraced by these women, most of whom I had never met, all of us there to gut ourselves, to lay ourselves bare on the page.

Food and wine and a raucous game of Cards Against Humanity knocked my mom's ghost out of me for the night, helped me feel more grounded in my own skin, fortified for the next day, our only full day of the retreat.

I spent much of Saturday pushing play, then rewind, then play again on the DVD player, making sure I captured every bit of dialogue from the documentary correctly, filling up almost my entire pocket-sized orange notebook with quotes about art and illness and death, lines like, "The family history is so profound that I think it's a story that has to be told, not just because it's my family but because of lots of people's families, who are dealing with this, who don't know what they're dealing with, who really need help in dealing with their doctors, and I think it's crucial to pay attention to these spirits that came to me to tell this story and it's, I think it's the hour of the moment of my life to be able to do this [nodding, closing her eyes as she starts to cry.]."

When it was time to go downstairs to join the women for our second and final dinner together, I had done very little writing but a lot of transcribing, and it felt like a fruitful day. My memoir had found a new form. It almost felt as if it had already been written in invisible ink, as if all I had to do was rub one of those magic white-tipped markers over the page, and the words would reveal themselves.

The dining room was bustling, the air thick with spice, when I arrived. I had been concerned that I wouldn't find much to eat at the pot luck—my doctor had encouraged me to cut gluten and dairy from my vegetarian diet, which often led to slim pickings outside my own kitchen. But there was peanut stew on the table, there was vegan asparagus soup, there was gluten-free pasta and the quinoa salad I had brought in my mom's black Dansk casserole dish. And the conversation proved to be just as delicious, just as nourishing.

After dinner, we all read from our works in progress, and I shared the new first page from my memoir. My heart raced the whole time I stood at the head of the table; by the time I sat down again, I was shaking. A friend across the table smiled at me and nodded slowly, as if to say, "Yes, yes, you are getting there." My heart raced in a different way as I listened to the other women read their brave, sexy, funny, profound works. Lots of gorgeous writing had been produced within those famously haunted walls.

When we talked about our writing goals for the coming year, a woman working on a memoir about being defrocked as a priest joked that she wanted to focus on combining poetry, contact improvisation, and klezmer music. "I love contact improv!" I piped up, and before I knew it, we were enlisted to give a performance. We all moved up to the ballroom on the second floor with our glasses of wine; I kicked off my shoes and soon found myself rolling around with my new friend, bearing one another's weight, letting her pull and spin me across the uneven wooden floor. I knew I would be sore, possibly bruised, the next day, but I didn't care—after sitting with words and ghosts all day, it felt so good to be in my body, to let my body slam and fly.

I finished transcribing *The Art of Misdiagnosis* the next morning. My feelings of anger had diminished. I had gotten more used to my mom's image, less shattered by it. The transcription had started to feel more like work, less like dredging my heart. And then another feeling crept up on me as I watched the film: admiration. My mom had made a movie, an actual movie. She had started to paint in her sixties without any training and then, at seventy, made a movie about those paintings, without any training. She had an idea, and she went for it. I had been too upset about the project when she was alive to see what she had accomplished. Now I could acknowledge what a feat she had pulled off. Even if much of the film was based in delusion, it was still a film, and she had made it. I had to bow to her for that.

Michael and Asher came to pick me up later that morning. As happy as I was to see them, it was hard to leave Saint Mary's, to leave these wonderful women and the support we had given one another as we wrestled with our own ghosts.

My little family spent a few hours in Virginia City—Asher panned for gold, fed a donkey carrots. We dressed up at one of those old-timey photo studios—Michael was a desperado; I was a "sexy cowgirl" with a corset and a duster. Asher was the sheriff who had locked us up in jail. The photographer slipped handcuffs around our wrists, put a rifle on Asher's lap. She was about to hand him a noose, "So you can string them up if they escape," she said, when I sucked in a sharp breath.

"Are you okay with that?" Michael looked at me with concern.

"No thank you," I told the woman, who quickly put the noose away. I was tempted to tell her about my mom but didn't want to start crying before she took our picture. Besides, she didn't need to know. Right after my mom died, I would blurt out, "My mom killed herself!" or "My mom hanged herself!" whenever someone called to congratulate me about the baby. I had no filters; it just barreled out of me, shocking unsuspecting friends and colleagues. I was finally able to measure the way I doled out information. Writing about her death gave me a valve—the story wasn't always ready to explode from my throat. And now the book was giving my mom a valve, too, giving her a voice long after she'd wrenched her own airway shut.

We drove back up the mountain, watched the desert scrub slowly give way to pine trees. This is where ghosts live, I thought, if there are ghosts; this is where the veil grows thin, in the places where one landscape bleeds into another within us, the ecotone between life and death, between the real and the unreal. The "tone" in ecotone comes from the Greek "*tonos*," meaning tension; a place where two landscapes are in tension with one another, but maybe we don't need to think of transitional zones as being rife with conflict; maybe we can think of them as places of connection, of transfiguration, the "tone" offering a complicated harmony. Places where the stories that haunt us wait for us to set them free.

arse poetica

(or, a shitty metaphor)

"HOW WOULD LIFE BE DIFFERENT IF WE PROCRE-ated with our hands?" my professor Kevin O'Neill asked in "Construction and Deconstruction of the Self," the freshman seminar for students enrolled in the Johnston Center, the alternative school within the University of Redlands. Kevin was always asking provocative questions: what if our backs were our sex organs—how would clothing and furniture change? What would we do if we woke up in a differently gendered body? One morning, he asked us whether we look in the toilet after we poop. Only one person in the class said no, saying he had evolved to a more spiritual plane. Kevin didn't believe him.

"We *all* look in the toilet after we poop," he said, "because it's something we created. Our bodies want to see what they have created."

Birth is often used as a metaphor for the creative process—I've definitely used it myself in the past—but it's a bit of a cliché, plus it's not accessible to everybody (make that every body). I can see how another bodily function could be an apt metaphor, too, one we all share.

As a popular children's book title reminds us, everybody poops.

Think about it. The creative process is a lot like the digestive process. We take life into our bodies. We let it travel through us. We absorb what we can. We express those things that need to come out.

Bear with me here. Let me bear down.

Sometimes poems and stories come out in a messy, smelly gush. Sometimes we are surprised by their colors, by the kernels of life embedded inside. Sometimes we strain and strain, and all that comes out is a little pebble of language, maybe nothing at all. Sometimes a piece of writing slides from our bodies, and we feel cleansed and light.

Does this make you uncomfortable?

Shit makes people uncomfortable.

I amicably parted ways with a dear former agent after she wanted me to remove any mention of Crohn's disease from my memoir. My complicated journey with illness as a young person—being seriously ill, then later pretending to be seriously ill because I didn't know how to not be "the sick girl"—gets to the heart of my relationship with my mom unlike anything else in my story. But my agent feared the bodily chaos in the book would make people uneasy. It made *her* uneasy, and she urged me to cut it. After dragging my feet for several months, I decided to listen to my gut and step away so I could write my memoir the way I needed to write it. I'm grateful she understood and gave me her blessing, grateful I found a new agent who understood and supported my vision for the book, and found an editor who gave the book a beautiful home.

Just before *The Art of Misdiagnosis* was released, I was eagerly reading an essay about medical memoir when I came upon this passage: "…inflammatory bowel disease, which threatens life, as well as its sufferer's sense of self and sexuality, has never found its way into a great memoir. It seems unlikely that no worthy writer has had these diagnoses. Maybe some conditions just aren't inherently memoir-worthy."

I can't say whether my memoir is "great," but I steadfastly believe we shouldn't declare any material from our lives unworthy of memoir—we should be able to talk and write freely about every aspect of the human experience, even the most disagreeable, shitty ones. If we don't, we perpetuate silence and shame.

After I had surgery to remove a length of obstructed small intestine, I devoured books by authors with Crohn's disease— *Meaty: Essays* by Samantha Irby and *The Man Who Couldn't Eat* by Jon Reiner, which both mine our shared illness for great comic and dramatic value, as well as Matthew Siegel's poetry collection *Blood Work*, and Chris Kraus's autobiographical novel, *I Love Dick*, which both address the authors' Crohn's experience with tremendous honesty and craft. These books made me feel less alone; they helped give me courage to take that part of my own story out of the shadows.

I consider all of them great. A book about any subject has the potential to be great.

May we give ourselves permission to write "shitty first drafts," to use Anne Lamott's phrase, and later craft them into beauty. May our writing be just as metabolic as our digestive system, just as transformative.

May we embrace all aspects of our lives in our work, including the parts that are uncomfortable and unsavory, the parts we're told to not discuss in polite company.

Polite is overrated.

Polite keeps us from our truth.

May we write words that still steam from the heat of our bodies. May our lives become rich, loamy, fertilizer.

Let's see what grows from the dirt.

self interview

how did writing your memoir change you?

I started to drink coffee and booze for the first time in my adult life during the writing of my memoir. There isn't a direct correlation—*The Art of Misdiagnosis* didn't drive me to drink—but it feels connected. I never regularly drank coffee or alcohol until I was forty-five—an age when many friends are cutting back on both. I started when my husband and I were separated, and I was feeling a little reckless, a little wild. Part of the reason I hadn't imbibed for most of my adult life is that for many years, I thought I had acute intermittent porphyria, a genetic metabolic disorder with a long list of contraindications, including alcohol, and my mother had me convinced a glass of wine could kill me. Coffee isn't on the forbidden list for porphyria, but when my first cup in college made me feel as if my bones were going to shoot out of my skin, I took this to mean I was too sensitive to enjoy caffeine. I believed this for decades. I had come to see myself as a fragile flower—a label I once took great pains to paste to myself, a label I've found challenging but satisfying to peel away. I still don't consume much of either, but drinking coffee and the occasional glass of wine has helped me see myself as an adult, helped me realize I am far sturdier than I had imagined. Writing *The Art of Misdiagnosis* did the same.

how did writing your memoir change you?

I started *The Art of Misdiagnosis* seething with anger. It seared the page like acid. This was good. I've always had trouble facing and expressing anger in my life, and it helped me greatly to give it voice,

to exorcise it from my body. One of the most satisfying dreams I've
ever had about my mom was a dream years before her death, where
I sat across from her at a restaurant table, opened my mouth as wide
as it could go, and bellowed, "NOOOOOOOOOOOO" like a fog-
horn, from the very depths of my body. The word roared on and on
and on and blew her hair back like gale-force winds. A Gayle-force
I never used in the waking world. I woke feeling so much lighter
inside. Writing my way through anger had a similar cleansing effect.
And much to my surprise, I wrote my way straight into compassion
for my mom, straight into a new kind of Yes when I thought of her.
By the time I was done writing the memoir, I appreciated my mom
more deeply than I ever had when she was alive.

how did writing your memoir change you?
It helped me see myself more clearly, my own patterns of silence
and denial, the times when I've been less than honest in my life.
I felt a lot of shame as I confronted these aspects of myself, but
I was able to find my way toward more compassion for my own
little self, too. And seeing my own patterns more clearly means it
will be easier to break those patterns. It has been already.

how did writing your memoir change you?
It helped me trust myself more. Trust myself enough to know
when I was avoiding a scene because I was scared and needed
to gently nudge myself forward, or when I truly wasn't ready to
write the scene yet and needed to give myself more time. Trust
myself enough to cut a full quarter of the text from the manuscript,
knowing I was bringing the memoir into sharper focus, knowing it
had been important for me to write those extra pages, but it wasn't
important for anyone else to read them.

how did writing your memoir change you?
It aged me. I don't know if I can blame that on the book

alone—blame time, blame Trump, blame major abdominal surgery, blame my dad's death last year, blame losing a lot of weight through illness, through nonsense, then gaining back more than I'd lost, blame not enough sleep, not enough exercise—but *The Art of Misdiagnosis* definitely carved new grooves into my skin, turned my hair whiter beneath the purple dye. I think about *Poltergeist*, or even the woman-centered *Ghostbusters* movie, where people's hair turns white after they return from some other dimension. I delved into my own shadowy places, and that journey is written all over me. A friend noted that I've been looking more alive lately, though, so maybe the memoir has changed me in that way, too. It's carved out more space for authentic joy.

how did writing your memoir change you?

In some ways, it ruined my writing life. I felt adrift after I finished crafting the memoir, lost as a creative person. I was sure I would never feel the same, terrible urgency to write again, that nothing I wrote would ever feel as meaningful or necessary. I was sure I had burned my writing self down to cinders, that I had nothing left to pull from, that all other writing would feel empty from that point, forced. But I am beginning to crawl out of that wreckage. I am starting to spark and simmer with new possibilities.

how did writing your memoir change you?

Less than I thought. I had deluded myself into believing I had healed myself completely by writing *The Art of Misdiagnosis*. I thought I had processed my mother's death as fully as I possibly could, that I had left no stone unturned inside myself, no emotion unexplored. And then grief, that sneaky asshole, found a way to sneak up and kick me in the throat again, and I was shocked. Shocked it was still there, even after I had written about it so thoroughly, shocked it still was able to lay me flat.

how did writing your memoir change you?

More than I thought. I feel braver than I ever have in my life. I have always been a quiet, shy person; writing this has made it easier for me to use my voice off the page—I am quicker to speak up, speak out. Perhaps part of this is growing older and giving fewer fucks, but I know writing *The Art of Misdiagnosis* helped me get to this point, too. The memoir helped me stop holding myself back as much. I no longer have the same tendency to hide, the same tendency to stay silent—or maybe I do, and I'm able to push past it now.

how did writing your memoir change you?

In addition to drinking, I've started swearing. *The Art of Misdiagnosis* has turned me into a fucking ruffian. Really, I don't swear all that much, just as I don't drink that much, but I don't cringe when I do it now; it feels fucking great when I do it now. The fragile flower is gone, and good fucking riddance.

how did writing your memoir change you?

It helped me gain some distance from my own story, knowing that once it goes into the world, it will not be my story anymore—it will be metabolized in a new way by everyone who reads it, will become their own. This feels like a fist unclenching inside my heart.

how did writing your memoir change you?

On a molecular level, I just feel different. I am letting myself feel proud of myself and my writing for maybe the first time. I've never been comfortable with the word "proud," at least not when it comes to myself, but I'm letting myself own it now. I did this thing I wasn't sure I could do. I made something out of this pain. I wrote the book of my fucking life.

dipping my mother's hair in ink

(or, on later doubts about memoir)

THE BOY WHO SAT BEHIND MY MOTHER IN PRIMARY school dipped the tip of her braid into the inkwell carved into his desk, turned her hair into a brush, slashing calligraphy across the back of her shirt, marking her with his intent. My grandmother told her to be flattered, said it meant he liked her, but did my grandmother worry about this boy, this ink, his intent? Did she scrub and scrub at her daughter's shirt, hoping it would come clean? Did it ever come clean? Did the ink wash out of my mother's hair, dark swirls of it disappearing down the drain, or did it seep deeply into each shaft, dyeing it until her mother trimmed off the ends, littering the floor with the intent of that boy? And where is it all now, that shirt, that hair, that ink, that boy, in what landfill, what house, what dust molecule? Have I breathed in flecks of it, that shirt, that hair, that ink, that boy?

When my memoir was published and interviewers asked how my mother would have felt about the book being in the world, shame crept over me, and I started to wonder: had I done the same thing as that boy? Had I dipped my mother's hair in ink, too, used her as an unwitting pen? Was I as complicit as that boy, taking what was hers and making it my own? Were my hands irrevocably stained?

Trusting the urgency of the creative process is one thing; holding on to that trust after publication can be another. While the book was received with overwhelmingly open arms and led to breathtakingly profound conversations, I also received Tweets like, "Shame on you" after an excerpt was published, and, "If I was your mother, I would kill myself, too." Of course, I am not alone in such trolling—it is sadly part and parcel of being a writer in the world these days, especially a woman-identifying writer—and I've received very little compared to many writers I know. But those posts got under my skin, fed the doubts and guilt already bubbling and growing inside me like a yeast.

What had I done to my mother? Was I that boy, that ink?

The question of how my mother would have felt about my memoir came up again at a university reading a few months after the book release, a reading in an actual castle on a campus in Pennsylvania, a space my royalty-hungry mother would have loved, and the same shame started to re-percolate in my gut. Then my gracious host said he sensed my mom would have loved seeing her face on the cover of my book, and I realized, yes, that's true— my mother always wanted to be the center of attention; she would likely have been thrilled to see herself on the cover of a book. Something relaxed in me at this revelation. And I trust that at her best, truest self, my mom would understand I wrote this book from a place of love, from a sincere desire to fathom her, to connect. If I've plunged my mother's hair into ink, I've also written her more deeply into my heart, tattooed her there, her presence now refreshed, indelible.

V

ORTHOPNEA:

breathlessness in lying down
position relieved by sitting up
or standing

shadow son

I HAVE A SHADOW SON—A SHADOW SON I DIDN'T GIVE birth to, a shadow son who believed I was his biological mother for more than a decade.

I first became aware of him in 2003, when a private investigator called. I had no idea what a detective would want from me—perhaps a bill collector was trying to track me down. Maybe my mother had hired him to find the fortune she believed my father was hiding from us. Over the years she had hired several people to find the money, to no avail, but none had ever reached out to me.

"Your son is looking for you," the private investigator said. "The son you gave away in 1985."

Now *that* I wasn't expecting.

"What?!" was all I could manage to say.

"Your name is on the birth certificate," he said.

I was seventeen in 1985, still a few months away from losing my virginity. I knew I hadn't given birth that year, but the call played with my head. Had I somehow blocked out an entire pregnancy? I started to feel disoriented as I pressed the phone to my ear, momentarily unsure of memory, unsure of reality. I wondered if this was how it felt to be delusional like my mother, although she always seemed so sure of herself, of what she thought she knew. I told the detective, no, it must have been someone else with my name; he thanked me for my time and hung up.

I didn't think much of this strange phone call until my shadow son contacted me himself via Facebook in early 2010. "This might be an insane question," his message began before he asked if I had given birth on a certain day in 1985. I had given birth to my youngest child three months before this message and was still recovering from both the birth and my mother's suicide.

I wrote back saying, No, I hadn't given birth in 1985, and wished him the best with his search. He apologized for any inconvenience and closed with, "Be well." I deeply appreciated these words; I felt far from well those days. I shut my computer and fell back into the utter immersion of mourning, of life with a newborn, figuring the situation was resolved.

But then I heard from him again, this shadow son. He assured me he wasn't seeking a relationship; he didn't want to derail my life—he had been having some health problems and wanted to understand his family medical history, he said. I was tempted to tell him how my mother had been working on a documentary about the various diseases she thought wracked our family, but that information would have no bearing upon his life.

I assured him once again I wasn't who he was looking for and thought the matter was put to rest until I woke to a notification on my phone in 2016, "Are you my Mother?" bright on the screen. I thought of the children's book, the little bird asking a cow and a dog and a steam shovel if they were its mother; then I read the rest of my shadow son's wrenching message, each word thrumming with pain. It gutted him that I wouldn't acknowledge him as my son, he said. It gutted me to read his words, to know he associated me with this deep ache, that I had become its locus. He was going to become a father himself soon, he wrote; if I was his mother, I was going to be a grandmother. I felt so helpless—I wanted to tell him I could be some sort of mother figure in his life, but I knew that wasn't the answer; he needed to know where he came from, and that wasn't me.

I offered to do DNA testing, write an article, do whatever else I could to help him find his mother, but he never wrote back; in fact, he blocked me. My shadow son instantly became even more of a shadow, and I was surprised by how this hurt—it felt like a hole in my life, a fresh grief. This man had projected so much hope and fear and anger and pain and confusion and love onto me, and I had let some of that seep into me, glimmer and rattle inside me as if I had a window into a parallel life, an alternate universe, where I had indeed given birth at seventeen. When he shut that window, my life felt smaller, somehow. Strangely bereft.

I found myself checking what I could on my shadow son's Facebook page to make sure he was okay. I knew he was the singer/songwriter for a band, one that was getting quite a bit of attention, and found myself visiting the band's website, reading his lyrics. Many are suffused with longing—romantic longing, yes, but I couldn't help but wonder if the lyrics stemmed from that more primal wound. I also couldn't help but feel a strange surge of maternal pride for his success. And when I saw pictures of his baby—my shadow grandchild—I couldn't help but kvell.

After I shared how haunted I was by my shadow son, my husband said, "Let's see if we can find his birth mother." My heart revved. In the fourteen years since the private investigator called, I had never considered doing this, but now it absolutely felt like the right thing to do. My husband and I launched into detective mode—I joked we were like Hart to Hart, those married detectives of seventies television; we may not have had their butler or yacht, but we had something they didn't: the Internet. Two different private investigators had pegged me as the birth mother, but within two hours of searching public records, my husband and I found a woman who seemed likely to be my shadow son's real birth mother, a woman whose name was very similar to my own but with a slightly different spelling, a spelling that matched a birth record from the day my shadow son was born. My heart sank when I discovered that this woman—who had come to feel like a shadow self, of sorts—had died in 2015, her name on a list of deaths of unhoused people in San Francisco.

I sent the links I'd found to my shadow son—who, it turned out, had unblocked me a few months before, in case I ever decided to reach out to him—and as we discussed this life-shaking information, we began to open up to one another. He told me when he was a child, he would spin in a circle, knowing at some point, he was facing his birth mother. I told him how I had come to think of him as my shadow son; he shared that he had written a song in the voice of his birth mother, imagining she was me, which he had named "Shadows." So wild that we had both used the word "shadow" in thinking and writing about one another; so wild that we could now step out of the shadows and into the light together, to see each other without that scrim of pain between us. He found relief in finally knowing the truth, even though it was tragic; I found relief in no longer having to carry his sorrow, in having transformed my sense of helplessness into real help. Within a day, my shadow son had found a biological sister; two weeks later, she attended his wedding. He had wondered where his baby's red hair came from; his bio sister has the exact same shade.

I recently spoke to my shadow son on the phone for the first time. It was wonderful to hear his voice, to have a real-time conversation, to laugh in recognition when he said, "We are probably the only people in the world with this particular relationship." A singular bond I'm deeply grateful for. He told me when his beloved father from the family who had adopted him was on his deathbed in 2012, he said he hoped his son would one day make peace with having been adopted. "He gave that to me, and you gave that to him," my shadow son told me. He said he'd never felt more a real part of the family that raised him than he does now; where he used to prattle to overcompensate, now he can sit with his family in what he calls "wonderful silence." "I'm not acting anymore," he said.

As we were saying goodbye, my shadow son said, "This may sound weird, but I love you, Gayle."

I answered straight from my mother-heart. I said, "I love you, too."

anniversary gifts

fourth anniversary: fruit and flowers (traditional, u.s.)

The morning of my fourth wedding anniversary, I banged my knee on the stationary bike at the gym. My skin purpled and swelled, tender like a plum.

Traditional gifts for a fourth anniversary are things with short lives; things easily bruised.

My husband and I had been separated for a month at the time of our fourth anniversary. I had been at the gym to try to get in shape for the man I was soon going to join at a writing retreat. I had been working hard to make myself disappear, although not the same way my mother had when she took her own life; I wanted to pare myself down to the bone, flare into new life, become a creature unencumbered by *kummerspeck*, or "grief bacon," a creature unencumbered by grief.

fourth anniversary: blue topaz (gemstone)

I came back from the gym and was reading student work in my new rental house, ice on my banged-up knee, when my husband swung by unexpectedly. Our three-year-old son, who happily split time between our houses, was at preschool; my husband had taken part of the day off from work to go on a coffee date with a woman he had met on an online dating site. He and the woman had talked at the coffeehouse for hours. He was all charged up, electric with it. They were going to get together again later that day.

I wasn't sure how to react. On the day we married, this was certainly not how I had expected to spend our fourth anniversary. I felt numb all the way through, as if the ice on my knee had affected my whole body, my brain, my heart. A spark of jealousy flashed somewhere inside my chest, but I tamped it down. I had no right to be jealous—I had put us in this situation; I had reached for someone else first. I told myself this could be a good opportunity to face my own jealousy, to find ways to let it go.

Jealousy had tainted my first marriage—my first husband had an affair early in our relationship, and I spent our whole marriage braced for it to happen again, a state that wasn't fair to either of us. I had made a vow to not fall prey to jealousy in this, my second, marriage.

As I mulled all this over, my husband swooped in and kissed me. I was too shocked to return the kiss, too numb. He pulled away and said, "I just wanted to see if the magic was still there. I guess it's not." I was still stunned silent when he let himself out of the house.

fourth anniversary: appliances, electric (modern)

I joined the dating site my husband was on, curious to see his profile. A friend helped me with the long sign-up process after our weekly two-ounce glass of moscato at the Mission Inn wine bar.

"What name should I use?" I asked, curled on my couch as she sat at my desk with my laptop. I felt loose and pleasantly tired from the small glass of wine and from the dance class that preceded it at my friend's creativity and wellness studio.

"How about Glittergirl?" she suggested. She was a big fan of glitter; I often wound up with sparkles on my skin and hair after I hugged her. I wasn't into glitter or makeup or anything else the name implied but gave her the go-ahead to type it in. I wasn't planning to use the site for anything but recon.

The name was already taken.

"What about Clittergirl?" I joked, sending us into a fit of giggles. It was available, so that's who I became.

"It's a superhero name," my friend said. "Clittergirl to the rescue!"

"The costume needs a hood," I laughed.

When we finally finished the exhaustive, exhausting questionnaire, the site offered a list of people I had matched with. I was shocked to see my husband at the top of it, nearly 100 percent compatible. His profile was earnest and thoughtful—he was studying to be a yoga instructor, was learning guitar, journeys he'd embarked upon after our separation. The photo he used was a cute one I had taken of him in a tree, looking up at the sky. I also matched quite highly with the woman he was dating, whose profile made her seem like someone I'd like to know. This offered some intriguing possibilities, but I was too invested in our separation and my romantic fixation to propose a threesome.

My Clittergirl inbox was quickly flooded with dick pics. I wondered if my gynecological username had emboldened this never-ending stream of propositions, but I learned from friends this was just part of being on a dating site. I didn't reply to anyone's advances; perhaps I wasn't cut out to be a sexual superhero.

Then Clittergirl received a sweet message. "I see we're a 98 percent match," it said. "Would you like to meet up and see what life has to offer?"

It was from my husband.

I could feel a corner of my heart thaw beneath the layers of ice I had erected between us, could hear, "He's a good man" whisper from that same place, but I quickly froze it back over and didn't respond to his message. I wasn't ready to let myself soften toward him, wasn't ready to let go of my stubborn pull toward this other man, even though I had begun to suspect I didn't mean as much to him as he did to me, a suspicion that soon played itself out during a trip together, and in his coldness toward me afterward. As I reeled from this rejection, I started to understand what I'd been putting my poor husband through.

fourth anniversary: linen and silk (traditional, u.k.)

Over the span of the next few months, I nursed my heartbreak, and my husband broke things off with the woman from the dating site after it was clear she wanted more than he was able to give her. We each slowly started to wallow less in our own misery, to work on ourselves more, started to grow stronger individually, more grounded, more at home in our own skin. (It helped that I had started to eat again, that I no longer wanted to disappear.) Eventually, tentatively, we started to feel more comfortable with one another again, too, even started to flirt a little.

On Halloween, after I had put our son to bed, my husband texted, "What will you give me if I come to your door?"

I texted back, heart pounding: "Everything."

He showed up a half hour later.

We were still cautious around one another after that passionate night and decided to take things slowly; we didn't want to let our physical connection blind us to the deeper connection and trust we needed to reestablish. As much as I longed to summon Clittergirl to the rescue, I knew I could only make amends as myself. It wasn't until around Christmastime that we were able to admit we had fallen back in love and wanted to do whatever we could to make our marriage work.

fifth anniversary: wood (traditional)

By the time our fifth anniversary rolled around the next summer, my husband and son and I were getting ready to move up to Lake Tahoe, a fresh start in a fresh place.

The traditional fifth anniversary gift is solid, utilitarian, something you can construct with. This fit; we were actively rebuilding our marriage, piecing it back together thoughtfully, slowly, crafting a structure we hoped could hold us both.

Historically, only the most impressive anniversaries were assigned specific gifts—as far back as the Middle Ages, twenty-five years of marriage was associated with silver, fifty years with gold. Then, in 1922, Emily Post suggested specific gifts to mark the first wedding anniversary, along with gifts for every multiple of five years up until the twenty-fifth; in 1937, the American National Retail Jeweler Association added gifts for the rest of the first fifteen years, as well as for every five years between twenty-five and fifty. "The order of gifts reflects the investment that the couple gives of themselves to each other," write Gretchen Scoble and Ann Field in *The Meaning of Wedding Anniversaries*.

sixth anniversary: iron (traditional, u.s.)

On our sixth anniversary, my husband and I—grateful for what truly did feel like 98 percent compatibility, grateful we took another chance on seeing what life had to offer us together—went down to the beach at Lake Tahoe to renew our vows and exchange new rings: titanium with a strip of blue stone to represent the place of our new beginning, the lake we now call home.

Titanium is similar to the traditional sixth anniversary metal but slower to rust. A substance that, like our marriage now, is built to last.

all that she wants

A SONG LODGED ITSELF IN MY HEAD, ONE I couldn't shake for weeks. Just one line of lyrics, really—the line about wanting another baby from Ace of Base's early nineties pop tune, "All That She Wants"—the same line bopping on repeat inside my skull. *All that she wants....All that she wants.... All that she wants....All that she wants...*

But I didn't.

I didn't want another baby, if I could even have one at forty-eight.

It had been way harder to recover from birth when I was forty-one than it had been when I was in my twenties. It had also been a huge adjustment to have a little being, heart-meltingly sweet as he was, needing me every second of the day again; I didn't have the same kind of energy I had as a young mother, plus mourning had complicated the whole postpartum period. As fiercely and deeply as I loved this baby (then seven) and my older kids, and as much as I'd gotten to a better place with my grief, the thought of starting all over again with a new baby made me want to rip my uterus from my body with my bare hands.

All that she wants...

When I told my husband this line was stuck in my head, he looked stricken. "Is there something you're not telling me?" he asked.

"I'm definitely not pregnant," I said. I was perimenopausal, in the middle of my period at the time. But then I saw his face cloud, saw him brace himself, and I realized the song could also mean "All that she wants is another lover." It makes sense that this would rattle him. "I am not interested in any kind of baby," I assured him. And I wasn't. I would never want to put either of us through that mess again.

All that she wants...

I once read a novel called *The Song Reader* by Lisa Tucker, in which a woman acts as a medium of sorts, "reading" the songs people have stuck in their heads, delving into these songs to reveal what's in their hearts, what they need to face. I tried to read my own earworm, tried to suss out any deeper meaning. One word kept jumping out at me: "wants." The word at the very center of the line, the very center of the argument, the very center of everything, really—want. Desire. Hers.

I had been thinking a lot about women and desire already. Joey Soloway's adaptation of Chris Kraus's autobiographical novel, *I Love Dick*, had just been released around this time, and both the novel and the television series it inspired were such rich explorations of female desire. In the series, which veers from the book in several ways, Chris, played by Kathryn Hahn, becomes obsessed with environmental artist Dick (Kevin Bacon), after she follows her husband, Sylvère, to Dick's institute in Marfa, Texas, where Sylvère will be a fellow at a residency for artists and scholars. Her desire leads her to write a series of searching, searing, erotic letters to Dick, an act Sylvère participates in, one that at first reignites their marriage but later dismantles it.

I read *I Love Dick* after my ill-fated affair imploded. I could relate to the book in so many ways—like Kraus's character, I had written a series of letters to the object of my obsession—mostly emails but a few real letters sent across the country, my tongue sweeping over the glue of the envelope. As with Kraus's character, my obsession began more as a crush on this man's writing, his way of being in the world, than on the man himself. Like Kevin Bacon's portrayal of Dick as a cowboy artist, this man wrestled with the elements in both his life and in his creative work, and this awakened something in me, jolted me from the slog of grief.

All that she wants....

Toward the end of my first marriage, my desire dried up, my body unresponsive. This was problematic—sex had been a central part of our relationship. I was too embarrassed to mention it to my doctor, too embarrassed to discuss it with my husband at the time, who I had been feeling disconnected from in other ways—ways I hadn't let myself fully acknowledge. I checked out books from the library on sexual dysfunction, hid them where my husband couldn't find them, pored through them to see if I could figure out what was wrong with me. When we started couples counseling, our therapist said, "Sometimes the body shuts down before the mind admits there's a problem." Our bodies are so wise; mine knew exactly what my rational self had been denying.

All that she wants...

When I fell in love with my second, current husband, my body woke up, roared. He would look at me and I'd get wet, something I hadn't known my body could still do. I was surprised by, grateful for, the intensity of my desire. It felt like a more deeply embodied desire than when I was a young woman, when a large part of the excitement stemmed from being wanted, from being able to see myself as a sexual being. My mind would often dissociate from my body back then, narrating my sexual experience instead of allowing a fulsome experience of it, sometimes in third person (*she is on top of him; he is kissing her neck...*).

In my forties, with my current husband and then with the object of my obsession, my desire became its own narrator, my body its own constant source of text.

All that she wants...

"I was born into a world that presumes there is something grotesque, unspeakable about female desire," Chris writes in one of her letters to Dick. "But now all I want is to be undignified, to trash myself. I want to be a female monster."

This line made me think of *The Laugh of the Medusa* by Hélène Cixous, in which she writes, "What's the meaning of these waves, these floods, these outbursts? Where is the ebullient infinite woman who...hasn't been ashamed of her strength? Who, surprised and horrified by the fantastic tumult of her drives (for she was made to believe that a well-adjusted, normal woman has a...divine composure), hasn't accused herself of being a monster?"

The wanting woman in the Ace of Base song is seen as a succubus; she's described as a hunter, evil sparkling from her eyes. A desiring woman is a threat. Our culture hasn't known what to do with her.

All that she wants...

I'd wondered at times if the flare of my desire in my forties was my ovaries clamoring for one last baby, shining their last beacons down the runway, singing their bold swan song. My sister-in-law told me her friend calls this "the zest," a final spray of juiciness from our bodies as fertility wanes. And it worked; that internal shimmer led to the light that is my youngest child. But I also don't want to reduce it to that. I don't want to reduce desire to our bodies' push toward procreation. That feels limiting, not to mention heteronormative. Not all bodies want to or can procreate; there are many types of sex between many combinations of bodies that could never result in pregnancy; we certainly can't pin this surge, this urge, to reproduction alone.

Hormones can, however, play a role. With some further research, I discovered that a drop in estrogen and a spike in testosterone can lead to a surge of desire in perimenopause. Oxytocin, the hormone that contributes to parents bonding with their babies, also dips, which some say can inspire women to shift their focus from caregiving to paying attention to their own needs. And trans women and nonbinary folx who choose feminizing hormone therapy will (sometimes after a brief dip in desire after starting estrogen), feel their desire become more aligned with their truest self. In *Me, Myself, They: Life Beyond The Binary*, Luna M. Ferguson writes about their experience with hormone therapy: "The hormonal magic running through my veins is now more hybrid, and this helps me be more comfortable with my sexuality, which I identify as queer, and to explore the edges of language relating to desire, attraction, and pleasure. My heart beats with a magnificent hybridity now; stretching out I feel more in-between, a little less trapped on one side of the binary and within my own body. My fluid gender is now matched with a transitioning towards my own story."

I keep finding more and more stories in which women make big changes spurred by unexpected storms of desire in midlife. Stories of women who discover—or finally let themselves claim—they're lesbian or bi or pansexual in midlife; stories of women who let desire guide them out of bad situations into the lives they truly want, toward their own most authentic, audacious stories.

Midlife desire often comes at a shock to these narrators, likely because such stories hadn't been told regularly in our youth-obsessed culture.

In *Harley and Me: Embracing Risk on the Road to a More Authentic Life*, Bernadette Murphy experiences a sexual awakening after leaving a long marriage, and finds herself, at fifty, "bewildered by the unrelenting nature of this drive I didn't anticipate."

Gina Frangello, in *Blow Your House Down: A Story of Family, Feminism, and Treason*, is similarly surprised by the force of desire that leads to an affair in her forties. "I had never felt the fragile pulse of my body's existence insist upon its will so primally before," she writes, "reducing all of whom I thought I was to an exposed wire of desire."

In her memoir, *Love and Trouble: A Midlife Reckoning*, Claire Dederer recounts how she is overcome by this "tidal, ridiculous lust" in her middle age. "I said it was like an old friend, but it's more like old weather, a particular kind of rain that hasn't rained in a decade."

In *The Madwoman in the Volvo*, Sandra Tsing Loh hadn't thought she'd ever want to have sex with anyone again, including her husband, but starts unexpectedly lusting after a longtime friend; "how interesting," she writes, "that it had turned out that at forty-six I wasn't entirely done."

Suzanne Scanlon's *Her Thirty-Seventh Year: An Index* is a meditation on a married woman's intense desire for a particular "man in boots." An understanding friend tells her that turning forty had led her to "a certain crisis point. I became convinced that I had to sleep with someone who was not my husband. It was the first time I saw desire so clearly, as an antidote to death, to mortality."

Was this at the heart of my own desire, at the heart of all these midlife eruptions of desire, something in us raging against death at a time when we start to feel our own mortality more acutely than ever? Something in us yearning to blaze brightly, to live our best lives while we still can? My yearning did help me climb out of grief, did help me feel fully alive again—so alive, at times, I felt my skin might burst. "Desire isn't lack," writes Chris Kraus in *I Love Dick*. "It's excess energy. A claustrophobia inside your skin."

The claustrophobia of desire longs for release, for liberation, for wide-open possibility. In her memoir in essays, *Tracing the Desire Line*, Melissa Matthewson writes, "I needed desire like I needed water, my shoes, my own breath. And more than desire...I needed freedom. I'm not special. This is not new, but it was new to me, so I broke everything I knew about myself and my marriage to discover how I could be a free woman."

All that she wants...

In her 1984 essay, "The Uses of the Erotic," Audre Lorde writes, "We have been raised to fear the yes within ourselves, our deepest cravings.... The fear of our deepest cravings keeps them suspect and indiscriminately powerful, for to suppress any truth is to give it strength beyond endurance." She writes about how we can reclaim that power when we let the erotic inform our life, our decision making, our creativity.

I understand Chris's impulse to turn her obsession into art in *I Love Dick*. It's the only way I've been able to integrate my own experience of limerence and its fallout into my self, my life. At some point, the man I had upended my marriage for sent an angry email, saying, "You need to stop writing about me." I wrote back something along the lines of, "I don't want to write about you. I *have* to." I honestly thought I was done writing about that time in my life, but the song stuck in my head sent me back to the page. A much less destructive impulse than that other obsession but perhaps no less dangerous.

"Our erotic knowledge empowers us," Lorde writes, "becomes a lens through which we scrutinize all aspects of our existence, forcing us to evaluate those aspects honestly in terms of their relative meaning within our lives. And this is a grave responsibility, projected from within each of us, not to settle for the convenient, the shoddy, the conventionally expected, nor the merely safe."

All that she wants...

I came to realize a state of arousal isn't always erotic; "arousal" can also mean being hyperalert because of stress or anger or fear. I was a bundle of nerves during the period of my obsession, constantly on edge, a jangle of light and heat and agitation. The second noble truth in Buddhism tells us all suffering is caused by desire and, as empowering as desire can be, this desire caused plenty of suffering. Suffering that still has ripple effects, ones I'm committed to facing, to repairing where I can.

All that she wants...

Of course, there is still much I want—so many stories I want to get on the page, so many books I want to read, so much change I want to see and work toward in the world, so much time I want with my loved ones (and so much health and joy I want for them)—but I feel settled in my own skin, my own life, and I'm grateful for that, for the peace that comes with that. Perhaps part of this peace is hormonal, now that I've crossed over firmly into menopause territory, but it also feels deeper than whatever's washing (or not washing) through my blood. This peace isn't a settling for the convenient or the conventionally expected; it's a peace open to the pleasures of the here and now.

If that song ever gets caught in my head again, perhaps I can convince my brain to change its lyrics, change them to words that more accurately reflect my current erotics: *all that she wants is what she has.*

press / pool

press (verb): move in a specified
direction by pushing
pool (noun): a readily available supply

THE WOMAN AT THE REGISTRATION BOOTH HANDS ME
a lanyard with two badges—a large plastic one that says MEDIA,
a smaller yellow paper one that says White House Press Pool.

White House Press Pool.

I feel giddy and guilty all at once.

When I heard on my car radio that President Obama was
coming to speak in the Lake Tahoe area, my heart went all fizzy—
Obama?! here?!—but by the time I rushed home to my computer,
tickets were sold out.

I was determined to find a way to get in.

A colleague told me more tickets were slated to be released that
Friday at four; I set a reminder on my calendar but had no luck,
despite refreshing Ticketmaster over and over at the appointed
time, assuring it again and again I was not a robot.

There had to be something else I could do.

I scanned the Lake Tahoe Summit website in desperation and
lit upon the "media inquiries" email; I have no press affiliation but
sent along my writing bio, named my husband as my photographer, and crossed my fingers.

It worked.

The woman at the media-registration table asks what outlet I'm with, and I'm not sure what to tell her. I'm an essayist, not a journalist; I have no idea who I'm going to pitch, what sort of story I might write about this event. "I'm freelance," I say, which is true, but I still feel as if I've conned my way here. I wish I could channel my mom's chutzpah—she would waltz into fancy resorts with her swim bag and use their "guests only" pools without compunction; she believed she belonged everywhere, deserved everything. Instead, I'm more like my dad, who once told me he felt sheepish taking an apple from a bowl in his own childhood home. Several years ago, I was able to bring my parents to see Bill Clinton speak at a publishing convention (where I also felt like a fraud, even though my publisher had flown me there to promote one of my books). My parents never stopped talking about that speech; they would have been overjoyed to see President Obama in person. They're both gone now, my dad just three months ago. I tell myself I need to push past my imposter syndrome and enjoy the hell out of this for them.

A dog sniffs my purse and Michael's camera bag after a Secret Service agent rifles through them both. Another agent asks us to each take a gulp of the smoothies we've brought with us, presumably to prove they contain nothing more nefarious than kale; we do, we're patted down, and we're in.

(I will later think about how it would not be this easy to get a press pass for a Trump event, seeing as how he considered the media the enemy—or, as Steve Bannon called it, the "opposition," saying the media should "keep its mouth shut.")

Press (verb): apply pressure to (a flower or leaf) between sheets of paper in order to dry and preserve it.
Pool (verb): to accumulate or become static

The Lake Tahoe Summit is an annual forum to discuss the future of the lake and how we can best restore and protect what has been called the "Jewel of the Sierra." Thousands of people are here; some, like me, are here mainly for Obama; some are here to see The Killers, who are taking the stage after the speakers; some are here primarily for the conversation about Tahoe. Lots of people have environmentally themed T-shirts and pins; others wear political T-shirts—lots of Hillary, lots of Dump Trump. I feel a bit overdressed—I'm in a maroon and black Diane von Furstenberg knockoff I found at Ross thirteen years ago. I wanted to look "professional" for the press pool, but I hadn't thought about how the synthetic fabric of the dress, the long sleeves would feel in the hot sun. Part of me wishes I had worn my "Give a Hoot, Don't Pollute" T-shirt instead.

Earlier, as we walked from our car to the venue, Michael and I passed a large, vocal crowd of Trans-Pacific Partnership protestors, and a pang sliced through my heart. It's been a long time since I'd been part of a protest. Other than circulating a lot of online petitions and articles and writing a few letters to people in power here and there, my activist side has been pretty dormant the last few years. I used to organize protests and vigils, used to put my body on the streets, on the line. What happened?

The protestors were chanting, "Obama, you can't run, you can't hide, we can see your corporate side," and I realized it's been a while since I've even been critical of our president. There are plenty of aspects of his presidency I haven't been happy with—his use of drones, for starters—but I'd been so focused on how much I love having a cool, brilliant, literary POTUS, how much I'm going to miss having him in office, I'd let the other stuff slide from my brain. My activist muscles have started to atrophy.

I guess I do know what happened. I've needed time to regroup, recover, rebuild after the storm of birth and death and personal and medical chaos in our lives. But I know people take to the streets even after they've been through much worse. I can make all the excuses in the world, and it's not going to help anyone—not even myself.

(I'll take my body to the streets regularly during the next administration, will help shut down streets at risk of arrest.)

Press (verb): forcefully put forward (an opinion, claim, or course of action)
Pool (noun): a small and rather deep body of usually fresh water

The pre-Obama speakers—senators Barbara Boxer, Dianne Feinstein, and Harry Reid, California Governor Jerry Brown, and Assistant Secretary for Land and Minerals Management of the U.S. Department of the Interior Janice Schneider—file onto the stage, and Michael joins the group of photographers being ushered to a closer spot.

The camaraderie amongst the speakers seems warm and genuine. Harry Reid says that after working together for more than thirty years, Barbara Boxer is like a sister to him. Boxer and Dianne Feinstein kiss one another affectionately each time they pass on the stage. And it's clear the speakers have a deep love for Lake Tahoe, that they are all working hard to keep it blue. I tell myself that as a journalist, I need to be objective, to be critical, to not get swept up in the feel-good emotion of all of this, but then I remember I'm not really a journalist. That maybe it's okay to feel good about politics for a breath or two, especially during this nasty election cycle.

The speakers remind us that while we're here to celebrate progress—the lake is cleaner than when Harry Reid organized the first Lake Tahoe Summit twenty years ago—we can't be complacent; there is still much work to do. Dianne Feinstein tells us Tahoe is getting warmer faster than any lake in the world; I can believe it—right now, the sun feels as if it's boring a hole through the back of my dress. Climate change poses a growing threat to the lake, making it more susceptible to wildfires, to invasive species; we must find ways to slow the damage.

Jerry Brown talks a lot about beauty, how beauty transcends politics, how the human imagination is so nourished by the beauty here, it inspires Democrats and Republicans to work together to save it.

(Not long after this, it will become hard to imagine Democrats and Republicans working together to save anything, not even democracy.)

Janice Schneider speaks about the importance of wildfire prevention; she mentions a law with an acronym pronounced "Sniblema," at least as I hear it—later I realize she's saying "Sniplema," for SNPLMA, the Southern Nevada Public Land Management Act, but it sounds like "Sniblema" over the speakers. A lot of people snicker when she mentions the name, and she laughs, too, assures us she didn't come up with it herself. I love it, though. I love it so much. It sounds like a word my dad would have made up. I can imagine him saying it in an exaggerated, Yiddish accent, splaying his fingers and sticking out his tongue for emphasis. Sniblema!

Press (verb): squeeze or crush (fruit, veg-etables, etc.) to extract the juice or oil
Pool (noun): something resembling a pool
<a pool of light>

Harry Reid starts to introduce Obama. "He has done more with his pen than any president to protect our natural resources," he says, and I get all fluttery. I love how Obama uses a pen—what a joy it's been to have a real writer in the White House, some-one who knows how to wield words with compassion and power. And then there he is, our president, on the stage in pale blue shirtsleeves, and I lose my mind. I scream and don't care how I look or sound, tears in my eyes. It's a good thing I've given up on journalistic objectivity.

"Hello, Tahoe," he says, and it's so cool to hear his voice in person, that familiar voice talking directly to us. "This is really nice. I'll be coming here more often. My transportation won't be nearly as nice, but I'll be able to spend more time here."

He's funny and personable; he uses great, concrete detail, great verbs—all the things I urge my students to do in their work.

(Unlike his successor, who says he has "all the words" but only uses a handful of them and never sounds as if he knows what he's talking about.)

Obama talks about how it's been said that if you're out in the middle of Lake Tahoe, the water is so deep and clear, it feels as if you're in a hot air balloon ("unless you're Fredo," he jokes. He's already mentioned that *The Godfather II* is his favorite movie; it's one of the reasons he's excited to be here). He talks about the Wašišiw people (Anglicized as Washoe), how Lake Tahoe is the center of their world, talks about how if this place is sacred to indigenous Americans, it should be sacred to all Americans. He quotes a Wašišiw elder who said, "The health of the land and the health of the people are tied together, and what happens to the land also happens to the people."

(Later, his successor will plow through water protectors to lay a pipe he has a financial stake in.)

Two women move into the aisle near the stage and unfurl a banner between them. I can see the paint backward through the fabric—"Keep our gas in the ground." I flash back to a time when I'd stood with Jodie Evans, cofounder of the women's peace organization CODEPINK, holding a banner between us that said, "Don't Buy Bush's War" during a speech by Congresswoman Hilda Solis. My heart hammered wildly when we disrupted her talk; I wonder if these women's hearts are galloping, too. It takes courage to interrupt a president. I send a beam of support their way, even as I'm eager for his talk to resume.

"I got ya," Obama tells them. "That's a great banner." He assures them he'll get to their subject soon.

(His successor, meanwhile, will tell a crowd to rough up a protestor during one of his rallies, saying it was the good old days when protestors would leave on a stretcher. Six journalists will be arrested merely for covering protests during the Inauguration. Republicans will be inspired to try to make protest illegal and GOP legislators will try to exempt drivers who hit a protestor with a car from any legal liability.)

"Conservation is more than putting up a plaque and calling it a park," Obama says, and talks of how conservation helps the land build resilience to climate change. Our conservation mission is more urgent than ever, he tells us. "We do it to free more of our communities and plants and animals and species from wildfires, and droughts, and displacement." I am utterly rapt, my writing in my notebook a jumble because I'm looking at him, not the page.

"Places like this restore the soul," he says. So do talks like this. By the time he leaves the stage, waving and smiling, I am crying again, full of resolve and hope.

(Before long, it will be hard to remember what hope feels like. It will come in fits and starts over the next few years, harder to access than before, glinting under layers of despair and disbelief and outrage.)

> **Press (verb):** squeeze (someone's arm or hand) as a sign of affection.
> **Pool (verb):** to combine (as resources) in a common pool or effort

As my husband and I walk to our car, we run into Janice Schneider from the Department of the Interior, standing on the corner, suit jacket draped over one arm. I am starstruck. Obama had said one of the best parts of his job is having relationships with people who do the right thing, despite the haters and the naysayers; he acknowledged all the people on the stage, including her.

"That was wonderful," I tell her. "Thank you for all you're doing."

"You're doing a great job here," she says as we shake hands. "Keep up the good work."

What am I doing? I wonder. Not enough. Never enough. I wonder if she thinks I'm someone else, if she thinks I'm doing something I'm not, something great, until I realize she must mean the collective "you," the people of Lake Tahoe "you." I vow to do more as part of that collective "you," that collective "us"; I vow to do more, in general.

After we head off in our separate directions, I am tempted to turn and yell, "Sniblema!" but manage to suppress the urge.

Press (verb): continue in one's action
Pool (noun): a quiet place in a stream

The road home hugs the lake, and I stare out at its expanse, note the way the colors shift—turquoise near the shore, a deeper blue near the center. Something in me relaxes when I see the lake; some deep part of me lets go of whatever anxiety I've been carrying in my body. I hold the Press Pool pass against my belly and take a deep breath, feel the badge move with me. I remind myself that my writing brought us here, to this beauty, something I need to remember when I feel like an impostor. My pen is, of course, not even remotely as mighty as Obama's, but perhaps my writing can find some small way to help keep this beauty alive. My activist muscles twitch beneath my skin. The sun sends a broad swath of sparkles across the water. The lake winks at us all the way home.

(My activist muscles will kick into high gear after the election—I will soon be calling my reps nearly daily, showing up at their offices, sending letters and making phone calls and canvassing neighborhoods, and more. I will realize I've given too much time and energy to self-doubt, to holding my tongue. I will press my heart, and action will pool out.)

VI

BRADYPNEA:
decreased breathing rate

room 205

(an essay in 205 word flashes)

the situation

It's one of those things you wouldn't believe in fiction—"too coincidental," you'd write in the margins of a student story—but it's true. Your dad lived in four different Room 205s, in four different facilities, over the last four years of his life. The first Room 205 was in Vista Knolls, a rehab center in Vista, California, where he recovered from hip surgery at ninety-two and slowly learned to use a walker. When he was well enough to be released, he transitioned to Room 205 at Sunrise, an assisted-living place near your house in Riverside, California. When that place felt too sedate to him, you moved him a couple of miles to Room 205 in Olive Grove, an independent-living community with the assisted-living services he needed. His final Room 205 was in Sierra Place, an assisted-living facility in Carson City, Nevada, after he moved with you to Lake Tahoe. No one requested this room number; it just kept offering itself to him, the only room available in each place. 205. 205. 205. 205. He's been gone for four years now, and you can't stop thinking about this strange numerical coincidence, can't stop wondering what all these 205s could mean.

the tours

You were given a tour when you first visited each place to see if it was worthy of your dad. Each time, you were shown the area they called "the café," the place where lemon or melon or cucumber slices floated in jugs of water atop credenzas, next to platters of cookies, sometimes bowls of fruit. You were shown the activity room(s), the activity schedule. All of them (except the rehab place) had balloon ball. All of them (except the rehab place) had bingo. Some places had lively lobbies; others were filled with quiet people staring off into space, some of whom reached for you as you passed. The dining halls smelled of canned soup; all of them (except the rehab place) offered you a free meal, pudding on every menu. At each place, you wondered how you could leave your beloved dad here; at each place, you saw people you hoped he'd befriend. A couple of places, you were happy to see, had book clubs, and lectures by visiting experts: on birds, on local history, on art. You told yourself you would offer a writing class at each one. You finally did at the last, where you learned about your dad's first kiss.

the first three 205s (the decisions)

Your dad's doctor gave you two options for local rehab places; you chose Vista Knolls because of the architecture, which felt more Jewish in some ineffable way—it had a cool, mid-century vibe, and lush landscaping—and the people who worked there seemed nice. The other place was a pink, faux-Mediterranean monstrosity; you couldn't imagine your dad inside it.

You chose Sunrise next (a name that seemed ironic, given all these folks are in the sunset of their lives, many of them sundowning, but the name felt hopeful, too) because your friend's dad had lived here and she spoke highly of it, and there was classical music playing and furniture in calm earth tones, and everything felt very hushed and safe. Your dad started there in a respite room to try the place on for size and eventually moved to a more permanent room, 205, although it turned out not to be permanent at all.

You chose Olive Grove at your therapist's recommendation, when you and your dad had a session to discuss livelier assisted-living options. Your dad liked the tropical vibe of the lobby, the buzz of the dining room, and the director, whose name was similar to your late mom's.

the furniture: part i

In the first, rehab 205, you left your dad's furniture in his Oceanside apartment because you hoped he'd be able to return to his life. Once he was in the second 205 and it was clear he wasn't going to be able to return home, you moved some of his furniture to his new studio space and the rest to your basement, set up a kind of ghost apartment there, a nice little seating area, as if he'd be able to walk down the stairs and live under your roof, something you longed for, something you looked into—how to make your house more accessible, angling a ramp up the front steps, turning part of the living area into a bedroom, installing a shower with rails in the bathroom off the kitchen. But he wouldn't consent to any of that. You tried and tried, but he always said no, always said he didn't want to be a burden, even though you insisted it would be an honor, a joy. You realized it would be a burden to him, though, realized he needed his independence, his space, his freedom to go to bed early, wake at midnight for a bowl of cereal, putter around in peace.

the last 205 (and a detour before that decision)

When you moved to Lake Tahoe the following year and your dad moved with you but didn't want to move in with you, he took a brief break from the 205s and lived in Apartment 295 (different only in the center digit) for a few months, his last stab at independence, although he couldn't really be independent—you hired a part-time caregiver, did a lot of caregiving, yourself, which of course you were happy to do. He turned ninety-five in 295; family came in from all over to celebrate.

When it was clear he needed round-the-clock care, his new doctor, whom you loved, recommended Sierra Place, a forty-minute trip down the mountain from your home. Not nearly as close as you'd like but close enough that you'd be able to visit often. Other than moments when you needed to race down the mountain, pulse clogging your throat, because he had a fall or other emergency, you came to savor that forty-minute drive. Each trip, you thought about the first time you took your dad to check out the place; he'd looked out at the expansive view of the lake and said, "I feel like my brain is giving birth."

the finances

You weren't sure how you were going to afford assisted living. The first 205 was covered by Medicare, but that stopped when you moved him to Sunrise. Your dad had outlived his term-life insurance policy (you'd much rather have him around than the money) and only had a few thousand in savings to supplement his monthly Social Security, so he couldn't finance it himself. You and your siblings planned to pool resources, but it wasn't sustainable for any of you; assisted living is expensive. You didn't know what you could do, but the director pointed you to a low-interest loan that would cover a few months, helped you apply for V.A. "Aid and Assistance" benefits for your WWII–veteran dad. Between those benefits, and the Social Security, his expenses were covered, with enough extra per month for him to treat you to an occasional meal out when he was up for it and even give his customary generous tip, sometimes up to 50%. Sometimes even more. He left some credit card debt after his death, and a collection agency hounded you to tears, but then *Last Week Tonight* did a segment about predatory post-death collections, and you stopped taking their calls.

the furniture: part ii

Both 205.3 and 295 were spacious, one-bedroom apartments that absorbed your dad's furniture as if they were waiting for each last stick of it. 205.4 was another studio, so you took most of his stuff down to a storage unit in Carson City. Your dad didn't need much in that last 205—his green recliner, his small table, two of his rustic wicker-seated chairs, some lamps, his collection of art, much of which came from your mom's brief stint as a corporate art buyer. You bought him a new daybed and bedspread, one that fit his Southwestern aesthetic, an aesthetic that puzzled you—where did it come from? He'd barely spent any time in the Southwest—but you were glad it made him happy. At some point, hospice moved in a hospital bed and raffled the daybed off to the staff with your blessing. After he died, you and your sisters chose the most precious things to keep—including the binder of his funny, moving personal essays and letters to the editor, and the notebooks full of what he called his "wonders" (among them, "I wonder if birds are ever constipated?" and "I wonder why clams are so happy")—and donated the rest.

the food

In the first 205, the food was so bad—a plate of what they called chow mein looked like a gray tangle of slime—you and your siblings, who flew into town in shifts, brought in food from nearby places. When you drove the two and a half hours to the next 205, you stopped at a fast-food place, and he said the chicken tacos tasted like freedom. He liked the salmon at the next 205, the fruits of the forest pie at the third 205, mostly ate microwaved turkey tetrazzini in 295 and the last 205, although sometimes he went to the dining room, and you regularly took him out to eat, wrestling his walker into your trunk. As he declined, he started to put strange things in his mouth on these outings—a lemon wedge at

Peg's Glorified Ham and Eggs, the tortillas still wrapped in plastic from El Pollo Loco. His favorite caregiver somehow got him to drink most of a strawberry milkshake when he was in and out of consciousness on his death bed, his last real food. Later, the hospice nurse told you she thought it's why he held on so long, that sweet, pink cream boosting his heart.

the catheter

Before your dad's hip surgery, the surgery that led to all these 205s, a nurse tried to insert a catheter; it took her a long time—his prostate was too enlarged to let it through. When she finally succeeded, the pee wouldn't stop coming; she had to keep getting new containers to hold it. You and the nurse looked at one another in disbelief as the pee flowed and flowed until eight liters—eight liters!—of urine sat in jugs outside his body. The little round belly he had been so self-conscious of settled back to flatness. The doctor said his bladder would never work properly again, so while your dad was still recovering from his hip surgery, he had yet another surgery to insert a suprapubic catheter that snaked directly out of his bladder through a hole in his belly and strapped to his leg. The catheter left him prone to infection. You learned in the first 205 that UTIs can cause cognitive changes in older folks, that the paranoia and confusion that had taken over him could be helped by antibiotics, and you were so grateful there could be such an easy fix, the kind you'd longed for with your mother's delusions.

the furniture: part iii

the week he was dying, you made a little nest of blankets and slept on the floor. When your siblings arrived, your sisters slept on the floor with you, your brother and sister-in-law at a nearby motel. The administrators told your family that you could sleep in the respite room down the hall, but you didn't want to be that far away from your dad (later, your brother was upset about this, saying it's not what your dad would have wanted, having all of you crowded in the room like that, that your dad was a private person, and your brother was right, your dad waited to die until you all left the room a few days later to go to a nearby Starbucks for breakfast). One night, you and your sisters stole the mattress from the respite room and slid it down the hall on its narrow edge, giggling and running on tiptoe like cartoon bandits, to your dad's room so you wouldn't have to sleep on the hard floor. Even so, it was hard to sleep—you listened to your dad's breath rattle like a coffee maker all night, holding your own breath in the space between his inhales and exhales.

the witches

You invited a rabbi to come to your dad's bedside, thinking it would be lovely for him to hear Hebrew, to have some spiritual guidance during his last days on earth. A woman who led a congregation in Tahoe City—a synagogue where you had attended a few services, going when your ancestry called you, as it did from time to time—drove all the way to Carson City, which you deeply appreciated. It was around Passover, the holiday of liberation, and your younger sister asked the rabbi if you could all sing "*Dayenu*," one of the traditional songs. You, your sisters, and the rabbi stood around his bed, heartily singing "Day-day-eynu" over and over as your dad, on some other plane, kept pulling his sheet to his mouth to try to eat it. At some point, you and your sisters realized it sounded like you were chanting "Die, die!" at him, like witches performing an enthusiastic spell, and the three of you couldn't stop laughing. "*Dayenu*" translates to "It would be enough." Forever wouldn't have been enough time with you dad, but it was enough to be with him, to laugh around him, to let him know how much he was loved.

the love: part i

You hoped he'd fall in love at every 205—maybe not the first one; he was just in survival mode there—but every one that followed. You held hope for the director of 205.3—not only did her name sound like your late mom's, but she was also funny, and she and your dad palled around and laughed together, but then she left. When he left the place, too, a woman pulled you aside and told you all her friends had been fighting over him, something he'd been oblivious to. At the final 205, a woman invited him to her room for tea; he seemed glad to have a friend but preferred time with his caregivers. The caregivers at every 205 loved him, often came to him for advice. You were moved by how he made everyone around him feel better, knew it would be his greatest legacy. You would have loved for him to fall in love, but you also knew his devotion to your late mother, even after her death, even though she believed he was hiding millions of dollars, believed he was trying to kill her, even though she, in fact, tried to kill him once, wouldn't let him consider this possibility.

the doubt

You wondered if you were doing the right thing at every single place, wondered if you were being a bad daughter by putting him in assisted living. Friends would say, "I could never put my parents in a home," and you would feel wave upon wave of guilt. You had looked into other options—you couldn't afford round-the-clock care, still couldn't convince him to move in with you. You tried to find a "home" that could really feel like home; none of them did, but all of them did, or at least came to, at least somewhat. He complained about all of these places—too many old people being the chief grievance—but he remembered each one fondly after he left, even seemed to have regret over leaving each 205 (except the first, rehab one), and you tried not to have too much regret, tried not to have too much doubt, but it crashed and crashed and kept crashing in. So did the worry. How could it not? You worried he was going to die in every single 205. You worried he was going to die in 295. You've worried about him dying in every place he's ever lived, even your childhood home.

the wild horse

You and your sisters stepped outside for a break, some fresh air. You'd forgotten life was continuing beyond the four walls of your death vigil and were shocked by the cacophony you found in the normally quiet courtyard. The assisted-living place was hosting an event celebrating a woman who'd traversed the entire state of Nevada on a once-wild horse (Nevada home to more than forty thousand wild horses, horses you'd seen around Virginia City, thrilled by their feral muscle.) The woman was there, as was her horse, as was her dog, as was a calf, and a sheep, and two tortoises that had just come out of hibernation the day before. Residents, staff, and guests milled and chattered, eating hot dogs, drinking cans of store-brand soda. You and your sisters plopped onto bales of hay, eyebrows lifted, and kept asking one another, "Where *are* we?" It felt as if you'd stepped into a David Lynch movie, some sort of surreal dreamscape. A bluegrass band featuring a blue stand-up bass offered the soundtrack from the gazebo. "I think *we* died," your older sister said as you stared at the horse, the bright blue sky above it festooned with cartoonlike, puffy white clouds.

the clothing

Your dad had always been a well-dressed fellow—his wardrobe consisted of many checkered button-down shirts, some jaunty sweater vests, a classy ivory linen jacket—though through progressive 205s, his sense of style and hygiene slid. He began to spend more time in pajamas and sweatpants, loose pants that made it easy to access the catheter bag strapped to his leg. In the end, he was wearing just a T-shirt, no pants or underwear or adult diapers, just a T-shirt slit below the crew neck, down the back, for easy removal. It gave your gentle dad a kind of James Dean look, a tough guy in a T-shirt, because he was tough, holding on to life with all his might. (And those were part of his last words: "With all of his might, mighty in mouth," words that seemed so biblical, you wondered where they came from, wondered if they were part of a Hebrew blessing, but when you did a search of the phrase, no match came up. A beat after this profound pronouncement, he also offered up these words: "Football team, football team," and yes, you were a team, huddled with your siblings, waiting for his final play.)

the love: part ii

You told him you loved him in every 205. You told him you loved him every single day, on the phone, or in person, or both. You told him you loved him when you and your sisters washed his wasted back after the hospice nurse said sometimes dying people want to be clean before they leave this life. You told him you loved him every time you slid a dropper full of morphine or Ativan into the space left by his missing tooth. When your mom died, so much was left unsaid, but that wasn't the case with your dad. You just kept telling him you loved him, even though he already knew. You told him you loved him when you climbed into his bed after his death, and his body was cooling. You never thought you'd be able to lie next to a dead body, to hug a dead body, but the hospice nurse gave you a good hour with him before she called the funeral home, and you and your sisters stayed with him and loved him up as best you could, these precious last minutes you'd ever spend with his beloved body in the world, kissing and kissing and kissing his face.

the pandemic

The pandemic hit four years after his death. You still missed your dad every day but found yourself relieved he didn't have to see the administration's bungling of its COVID response, relieved he didn't have to witness the fascism he fought against in WWII creep into his own country, relieved (so deeply relieved) you didn't have to worry about him being quarantined, didn't have to worry about him dying of the virus. You saw social media posts of friends not being able to visit their parents in assisted living, of friends visiting their parents through windows of assisted-living facilities (sometimes using construction lifts to get up to windows on higher floors), of friends attending their parents' funerals via Zoom, grieving without the physical comfort of loved ones nearby. You were grateful for all your visits in all those 205s, grateful for the week you spent sleeping on his floor in that final room, grateful for hugging his cooling body. You wondered who was currently living in that 205, wondered who was worrying about that person. You worried about the person in 205, worried about all the people in all the 205s your dad graced, worried about all the people in all the numbered rooms.

the numerology

In the last 205, your dad on his deathbed, your family eating take-out Mexican food on his carpeted floor, you marveled yet again about the uncanny coincidence of all those Room 205s, trying to figure out what that could mean. Your sister-in-law, mashing avocados and salsa into guacamole, said in numerology, 205 is a seven—2+0+5. "Seven is a spiritual number," she said, and that made sudden sense to you, that series of 205s leading him out of his body, coaxing him toward spirit. You looked at the sealed door set into the wall by his bed, the door whose knob was removed just before your dad moved in, when the facility changed a double apartment back into two studios, leaving a flat, silver disk where the knob had been. You thought about the door he was about to pass through, not the door marked 205 that led to the hallway that led to the elevator that led to the lobby that led to the world, but the door marked 2+0+5 that led out of this world, the one whose knob was still invisible to you, the one that shimmered before him, the one only he could see.

my parents' delusions

MY DAD THOUGHT MY NOSE WAS A BABY. HE SAID there was a baby on my face, where my nose should be; a full body and a head. He found it funny. He wanted to take a picture so I could see what he saw.

❧

My mom thought my dad was hiding millions of dollars from her, from us. She thought he was part of an international money-laundering scheme.

❧

My dad called as I drove to pick him up to take him to the dentist. "I can't make it to the appointment," he said. When I asked him why, he said, "I'm in Bosnia." Apparently, he had been in Bosnia for the last five days. He told me he'd received a voice-mail message from himself saying he was lost in Bosnia, but he wasn't afraid. When I got to his room at the assisted-living place, he wanted me to listen to his voice mail so I could hear the message. Even though I doubted the message would be there, part of me wondered if he did somehow call himself, if I could hear what he heard. But no, when I pressed play, all I heard was myself, a message I had left a couple of days ago, the little-girlishness of my voice making me cringe. Later, he shook his head and laughed a bit, saying "Bosnia," stunned by his own brain. When I brought up the story a few weeks down the road, he said earnestly, "It wasn't Bosnia. I was in the Bosporus."

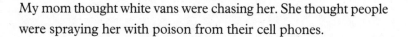

My mom thought white vans were chasing her. She thought people were spraying her with poison from their cell phones.

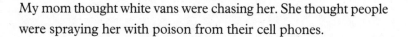

My dad thought President Obama had asked him to be the new leader of the civil rights movement. He thought the FBI had transported his whole apartment to Washington, D.C. "I'm going to be a hometown hero," he told me excitedly.

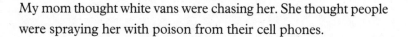

My dad's death certificate reads:
"IMMEDIATE CAUSE
(a) Cardiopulmonary Failure
DUE TO, OR AS A CONSEQUENCE OF
(b) Debility and Decline
DUE TO, OR AS A CONSEQUENCE OF
(c) Senile Degeneration of The Brain
DUE TO, OR AS A CONSEQUENCE OF
(d) Dementia, Vascular"
My mom's reads: "HANGING BY ELECTRIC CORD FROM PIPE." (Clearly, there are no capitalization standards from

coroner's office to coroner's office.) It doesn't say "DUE TO OR AS A CONSEQUENCE OF Paranoid Delusion," but the subtext is written all over the page.

‹›

Watching both parents lose their minds doesn't give me a lot of faith in the future of my brain. My mind already feels slower than it once did, less electric. I find my memory fading, too; sometimes it feels as if the grooves in my brain are smoothing over, erasing stories trapped in each cleft, a sort of reverse evolution, turning my cerebellum from prune to plum, something firm and blank and tart.

This terrifies me—if I lose my memories, my stories, who am I? I feel panicky when I think of my childhood, my children's childhood, being lost to me forever. But maybe a sense of peace comes over people who lose all their memories. If we forget everything, every moment would be brand-new. We could just be like a nonhuman animal, or a plant.

I can remember lying in bed nursing my baby shortly after my mom hanged herself. I remember thinking I should be doing something more, something active, writing or researching or doing one of the many practical post-death tasks that needed taking care of, but then I thought about sows, about how a mama pig just lies on her side nursing her piglets, how that's all she needs to do, that's her task, she gives herself to it fully, and I let myself drop into that surrender, let myself just be a mother animal nursing her young—mind blank—and I found there was something comforting, liberating, in that. Maybe that's what it feels like to have your memory erased—you can just be a mammal in your body, living from moment to moment.

In her memoir *Ongoingness*, Sarah Manguso writes, "My goal now is to forget it all so that I'm clean for death." But I have to remember that's just memory loss. Delusion is a whole other story. Dementia is a whole other story. And after watching my parents, I know I can't take my lucidity for granted.

My mom, in her delusion thought everyone was against her. My dad had his own moments of paranoia and disorientation, but his delusions were more often of the absurd, even sweet, variety. I know I have no control over the matter—over that tender, amazing, convoluted gray matter—but if I have to lose my mind, may it be in the way of my dad. May I say things that make my family laugh and shake their heads instead of trauma-tizing them. May I travel to surprising places without leaving the room, see whimsical things, imagine myself a hero—which sounds quite a bit like the writing life, come to think of it, just without the mediation of the page. Maybe it would help to think of it that way, to think of delusion and dementia as a new way of living inside a story, entering nonlinear, unpredictable narrative. A way of life in which we let go of chronology, let go of traditional plot and sentence structure. That makes it sound less scary to me, makes it feel more like art than ruin. But I also know how scary it can be to get trapped inside a story—I saw that in my mom, how terrified and alone she felt in her delusion, especially at the end. Story can save us, but it can also imprison us. My mom may have killed herself to kill the story that had taken over her life.

My mind wants to create a happier narrative for itself—one in which it can avoid my parents' fate, one in which it can hold on as long as my body does, one in which my body and mind stay vitally, inextricably linked, until they both give up the ghost—but at the same time, my mind knows it may not be the final author of my life.

In my poem "Last Words," I write that I hope my last words will be "I love you." I still hope for this. If my mind unspools, my dear ones, if strange last words fly from my mouth at the end of my life, please know what the deepest, truest part of me wants to say...

my love for you, for the world, riding
my last breath—*I love you*
I love you I love you.

eating the food
of the dead

THE LAST DAY I SAW HER ALIVE, MY MOM LEFT A
bottle of Snapple in my fridge—diet peach iced tea, the kind
with "Real Facts" printed inside the cap (for example, "Real Fact"
#776: "More babies are born at night than during the day"). I had
given birth at 10:33 at night just two days before. My mom carried
Snapples around with her because in those days, she only trusted
sealed beverages, only trusted prepackaged food. She thought
numerous people, including my beloved father, were trying to
poison her. Her perception of "Real Facts" was wildly different
from anyone else's, deserving of the quotation marks the beverage
company put around the facts inside its lids. She believed she was
being persecuted, being chased, believed these were the most "Real
Facts" in the world. I could barely stand to look at her bottle of
iced tea after we got news of her death. I avoided it in the fridge
like the poison my mother had been so afraid of, something too
caustic to touch.

("Real Fact" #722: The peach was the first fruit to be eaten
on the moon.)

Less than a month after my mom's suicide, my mother-in-law
came over to make Christmas dinner. I was hiding in my dark
bedroom with the baby, not feeling up to a visit, but she barged

in and insisted I join her and my husband at the table. She could be a difficult woman, snippy and intolerant, and she had never acknowledged my mother's death to me directly, not even one word of condolence, but I could tell she was trying, in her own way, to be kind. She was from Denmark and let me know she had made a few of her favorite Danish dishes—cucumber salad, new potatoes cooked with parsley, a huge vat of red cabbage.

("Real Fact" #822: The only jointless bone in the body is in your throat.)

"The cabbage might give the baby gas," I told her, worried about it coming through my breast milk—I was in a constant state of worry following my mom's death—but she *tsk*ed at my concern and said red cabbage was traditionally given to new mothers to encourage milk production. I scooped up the baby and tentatively ventured out of the bedroom, the light of the rest of the house stinging my eyes. The cabbage smelled awful but tasted quite good, stewed with vinegar and sugar. We still had a heap of it in our freezer when, less than three months later, my mother-in-law died of a sudden heart attack.

("Real Fact" #302: Ketchup was once sold as a medicine.)

Reeling with grief, my husband and I carried my mom's Snapple and his mom's cabbage with us when we moved into a new house and put them in the extra fridge/freezer in our new basement. They hunkered there like bitter talismans. I could feel them underneath us as we moved through the house. I didn't know what to do with that tea or that pungent, cruciferous tangle—it felt wrong to ingest them, wrong to throw them away. They sat in silent reproach, like our mothers with their arms crossed, angry at being ignored.

("Real Fact" #351: Cold water weighs less than hot water.)

On the first anniversary of my mother-in-law's death, in 2011, we decided to heat up a portion of the red cabbage in her honor; my husband choked down a few bites in tears and pushed his plate across the table. After we sold our house in 2014, we threw away the remaining cabbage, and I finally popped open the bottle of diet peach tea. I took one swig, cringed at the sweet chemical punch of it, then poured the rest down the drain. I didn't even check to see what was written inside the cap. The only Real Fact I knew at that moment was that I was ready to let go of the bottle and all it held.

("Real Fact" #62: The lifespan of a taste bud is ten days.)

My father's freezer was full of frozen Stouffer's dinners when he died—turkey tetrazzini and escalloped chicken and noodles. His last stabs at independence.

("Real Fact" #416: Many butterflies and moths can taste with their feet.)

One evening, our dad—comatose a few feet away—my siblings, and I decided to heat up these frozen meals for ourselves in his honor. I've been vegetarian since I was sixteen, and had cut out gluten and dairy a couple of years before for health reasons. But the escalloped chicken and noodles had been a favorite treat when I was a kid—back when my mom would bake it in the oven in its foil container, and the breadcrumbs on top would turn crispy and golden—and I fished out the pieces I could eat, the tender slices of button mushroom, the soft, saw-toothed slivers of celery. I wiped away as much of the creamy, chicken-brothy sauce as I could, but I could still taste it, and it transported me back to my childhood kitchen table, full glasses of milk and water in front of me, both parents healthy and smiling and alive.

("Real Fact" #364: Borborygmus is the noise that your stomach makes when you are hungry.)

Because of my dietary restrictions, I couldn't eat much of the food my dad left behind, his favorite Pepperidge Farm raspberry thumbprint cookies, the marionberry ice cream in his freezer, the fun size Snickers bars he kept in a bowl for caregivers and other staff, the English muffins he loved to eat with apricot jam and almond butter. I ate what I could—the almond butter straight from the jar, the tins of cashews, the stiffened prunes. I wanted to eat all of it, to taste everything he had loved on this earth.

("Real Fact" #714: When thirsty, a camel can drink twenty-five gallons of water in less than three minutes.)

At the celebration of my dad's life a couple months after his death, we made his favorite sandwich in the kitchenette of my sister's hotel room—toasted rye with mayonnaise, Swiss cheese, and bread-and-butter pickles, forever to be known as a "Buzz sandwich"—and cut it into small squares. We divvied his ashes into paper lunch sacks, one for each person present, then added the squares of sandwich. Everyone wrote messages to him on the bags—some of us included quotes from the "wonders" he had filled notebooks with since his retirement at eighty-five—and headed down to the same Oceanside pier where we had released my mom's ashes seven years before.

("Real Fact" #782: The human jaw can generate a force up to two-hundred pounds on the molars).

Real Fact: As per my dad's request, we played Louis Prima's "Enjoy Yourself, It's Later Than You Think" through the little speaker in my phone and danced together on the pier.

("Real Fact" #25: The only food that does not spoil is honey.)

Real Fact: We cast the bags to the water and watched them drift away, sending him off with the food of the living.

a mourner's guide to home renovation

YOU CAN BARELY SEE THROUGH YOUR SAFETY GOG-gles, the plastic fogged with heat, your eyes a teary blur. Your face is wet beneath the paper respirator, too, breath condensed against your skin. You bang a hammer against a pry bar, feel a piece of floor tile chip away. Not the same satisfying release as when a tile lifts whole from its moorings, but still, progress.

Still, grief.

Your dad will never see this house.

You remember crying the last time you and your spouse bought a house, too, crying because your mom would never see it. She had left you some money, money that paid for those renovations. Your dad left a little, too, very little, but it's helping; you'll put the rest of the renovation costs on a credit card, grateful you were able to get both houses for no money down, a benefit of your spouse being a veteran (it's still hard for you to believe your peaceful spouse was ever a veteran).

It's a strange coincidence, buying and renovating a house around each of your parents' deaths. You and your spouse made an offer on your first house a few weeks after your mom died by suicide; your dad was in a coma when you signed arrow sticker–marked lines of escrow papers, in your own fog, next to his bed.

You're still in a fog, but at least now you can break things. With your first house, you put your vision into the renovation but didn't get splinters in your hands, didn't feel walls give against your weight. Your spouse did the demolition then, tearing down cabinets, dismantling toilets and the disgusting shag carpet around them. You stayed back at your rental house with your baby, worried about noise, dust, fumes, worried about everything. You became a germophobe after your mom's suicide, a fearer of stairways you could fall down, bathtubs the baby could drown in, cords that could cause strangulation. Your body hypervigilant, constantly bracing itself for the next disaster.

This time, you don't have a newborn to fret about. This time, you go into the house whenever your son, now six, is at day camp and your spouse is at work. This time, you rip every inch of god-damn carpet off the floor yourself.

You are committed to doing as much demolition as you can now, as much of it alone as possible. It helps to be alone. You can smash and shatter and tear and bang as loudly and recklessly as you want. You can let yourself and your muscles scream without scaring anyone, except perhaps your new neighbors.

You pry more tiles off the floor, yank up tack strips, aware you are undoing someone's hard work, their dreams for this house. You know someday someone will undo all the work you will pour into this space now. This house will outlive you and your mark upon it. Still, you feel an unfamiliar, welcome surge of power when the baseboard pulls cleanly off the wall, nails popping out one after another, pleasurable as vertebrae cracking during a twist or a good hug.

A few days after your dad died, the day after your sisters left town, you had to attend the inspection for this house. You weren't ready to face the world, but your spouse was at work, and one of you needed to be here. Your real estate agent had known your dad—his wife was one of your dad's caregivers; their family had joined yours on a catamaran for your dad's ninety-fifth birthday. He gave you his condolences when you arrived, and you lost it, sobbing against his shirt. You pulled yourself semi-together by the time the inspector showed up, but your body was still like jelly—jelly electric with frayed nerves. You longed for some sort of armor, some new, protective skin.

Maybe that's what this house is for.

Some of the baseboard is stubborn; some of it breaks off in pieces, requires extra force. Some of it is so stubborn, you leave it for later, for a time when you hope you'll feel more strength. It seems to be especially stubborn near corners and around doorways, the nails holding on for dear life. You don't usually have the mouth of a sailor, but you swear at the baseboard, kick at the door.

In another weird coincidence, this house has the exact front door as the first house you and your spouse bought, one you haven't seen anywhere else—slightly medieval looking, solid wood, with a small, hinged square at the top; you want to say, "Hark, who goes there?" whenever you open it and peer through its iron grate. Everyone who comes by the house comments on the door, but you can't wait to replace it, to have a door you'll be happy to open. This door is like a portal back to bad times.

Your marriage imploded inside that other house. The main things that kept you going during that time were your beautiful boy and your home renovation. Thank goodness for babies and fixtures—they fix you to this world. Unfortunately, they didn't fix you and your husband to one another, though you reconciled after six months apart, around the same time you were invited to be a writer in residence at a college in this beautiful mountain village. A deus ex machina stroke of luck. It feels like a do-over of epic proportions even though this new house is a third the size of the one you renovated before.

That house had been a faux mountain lodge plunked in the middle of the desert—large, funky photo murals of the forest on many of its walls. Now you can look out your windows and see a real creek, real trees. Maybe your other house was preparing you for this one. Maybe your other grief was preparing you for this one. Grief from death by natural causes is simpler than grief after suicide, you find. Not easier but simpler. Purer. Like the clean mountain air all around you. Like the clear, cold water of the lake.

You fail to wedge the pry bar behind a new stretch of baseboard, tearing a patch of paint from the wall, and it suddenly hits you: you're an orphan now. The thought has occurred to you before, but you'd dismissed it—a middle-aged woman shouldn't call herself an orphan, should she? Still, you feel it now, in every cell of your body. It hits you so hard, you drop your tools and crumple to the subfloor, tile grit encrusting your sweatpants. You shove the goggles up onto your forehead, pull the respirator from your mouth, try to catch your breath. You are crafting your own orphanage here, you realize, tearing everything apart so you can create something new, a place where you can try to figure out how to raise yourself. You tilt your head toward the beamed ceiling, high and peaked above you. The house is small, but there's plenty of room for grief. For ghosts. You let dust fall upon your face, the house speckling you with its restoration, marking you, making you its own.

VII
APNEA:
absence of breath

figures

TWO BITS OF RECENT NEWS CHILLED ME MARrow-deep: my childhood skating rink is going to be torn down, and Madrid is using a skating rink as a makeshift morgue for coronavirus victims.

I skated at Robert Crown Ice Arena in Evanston, Illinois, most days after school; some days before, too, if a competition was coming up or I had an extra session with my coach. An hour of Figures, slowly etching giant eights onto the ice, then an hour of Freestyle, when I could blaze across the rink, leaping and spinning and practicing my routine du jour. That whole building is so alive inside me—the brown, speckled rubber floors, the large, square benches covered with carpet, cubbies beneath for our shoes, the scent of hot dogs rolling under a heat lamp in the snack bar, the way the frigid air burned my nostrils when I neared the ice, the satisfying groove a blade carved after a clean jump. I could draw you a map of the building, offer a story or sense memory for every square foot. My mind can barely comprehend it not being in the world.

It's March 2020, and my mind can barely comprehend what's happening in the world, in general, all these mounting figures, bodies laid out on a Madrid rink that once teemed with grace and speed. I wonder how many of those people had figure skated at this very rink, had fallen or soared within its walls, how many of them had laughed there, not knowing someday it would be full of corpses, that they might be among them.

I think about where I live, North Lake Tahoe, and wonder where mass amounts of bodies could be stored. We've had a mild winter—all the outdoor seasonal rinks have closed—but snow has been falling in earnest again lately; it's made our quarantine feel all the more surreal, as if we're sheltering in place inside a snow globe. While it's more likely that a temporary morgue would be set up in the casinos or convention center down the mountain in Reno, I find myself imagining corpses lined up in the snow at nearby Mount Rose Meadow like fish on beds of crushed ice. I wonder who I'd know among the bodies, wonder if my own body would land there.

My mind keeps spiraling toward death—how could it not?—and I think about death spirals, those risky moves done by pairs figure skaters, in which one skater plants a toe in the ice and pivots around, holding the hand of their partner, who arches back until they're spinning in a nearly prone position on one foot, hair often brushing the ice. I think of all the hair resting on the ice in Madrid now, all the heads of the dead, years of memory and experience frozen within them. I think about Zamboni machines, how they clean the ice between sessions, spraying water to melt away the gouges and scratches and piles of slush, freezing it all back into a smooth, glassy sheet. But Zambonis can't always erase everything; some divots and scratches are too deep to fill, some bumps too tenacious to shave. I wonder if anyone will ever skate in that Madrid rink again. I don't think I could—I wouldn't be able to get all those figures out of my head, the weight of all those bodies, the silenced lives and stories within them. Maybe people should only skate figure eights there in the future, sketching the symbol of infinity with the thinnest edge of a blade.

I never really liked the Figures hour of skating practice—I much preferred the thrum and rush of Freestyle—but I look back on it and it seems so soothing, so meditative, that slow, careful tracing. I long for it now. I can feel myself there again on the doomed rink of my childhood, cold air in my lungs, making circle after patient circle, leaving a mark so faint, you'd have to kneel to even know it was there.

rib / cage

(a meditation in twelve bones)

(The seeds) remember what their god whispered into
their ribs: *Wake up and ache for your life.*
—*Natalie Diaz, from "Postcolonial Love Poem"*

1. (true rib)

I've been sick for several weeks—presumed COVID—and am
now dealing with what my doctor thinks could be post-viral
costochondritis, an inflammation of the cartilage between the ribs
and around the breastbone. I've never been as aware of my ribs as
I have these last few weeks—they grump at me with every breath,
sometimes through pain, sometimes by resisting each
inhale. They've never felt so much like a cage,
my lungs large, pulpy wings
trapped inside.

2. (true rib)

The rib cage is also called the "thoracic basket"—I love how
these words sound together, that hiss in the middle of each
thorassssic bassssssket. My basket is made of concrete
and steel. My basket sometimes feels full of
wet muscle, sometimes venomous
teeth.

3. (true rib)

"Maybe you've cracked a rib," a friend says, telling me she cracked
ribs coughing when she had a bad case of flu. She said it felt as
if there was a band around her chest, and it does feel like there's
a band around my chest, too, tight and strong, but in
the X-ray, my ribs look fine, ghostly fingers
splayed beneath my
skin.

4. (true rib)

We have seven "true" ribs, three "false" ribs, two "floating"
ribs. The true ribs span from spine to breastbone; the
false connect to the breastbone via cartilage, the
floating attach only to the backbone, their
fronts hovering inside our
bodies, free.

5. (true rib)

I've taken two courses of antibiotics during this illness, a short course
of steroids, used two different inhalers, and a nebulizer, but the
thing that's helped most is my husband rubbing my ribs. He'll stand
behind me and run his hands up and down the sides of my rib
cage, fast, as if he's playing "Flight of the Bumblebee" on
a washboard, and a riot of pain and pleasure rico-
chets through my body. When he removes
his hands, my ribs continue
to pleasantly
burn.

6. (true rib)

Each rib has three parts: a head, a neck, a shaft. It makes me
think of Eve being made from Adam's rib—that head and neck
and shaft; no womb, just hard bone. This myth has
always irked me. I rename the parts of the rib
to my own liking—lip,
crest, curl.

7. (true rib)

My father cracked one of my mother's ribs on one of their early
dates. He was lifting her into a boat for a tour of Lake Michigan
off the shoreline of Chicago and his oarlike thumb snapped
the delicate bone. The only time he ever physically hurt her,
although she would claim otherwise decades later in the
grip of paranoid delusion. I wonder if her rib
healed properly, if it ached when
I was growing
beneath it.

8. (false rib)

The Sumerian word "ti" means both "rib" and "to live"; the
Sumerian goddess of life, Ninti, was birthed to heal the rib of
Enki, the god of creation, after he had eaten forbidden flowers.
Some people believe the Adam and Eve story stems from this
myth. Some people who believe the Adam and Eve story think
men have one less rib than women, but this isn't true. We all
have twelve pairs (except for the occasional human
who has what's called a "gorilla rib," a thir-
teenth pair, like those in the animals
we evolved from.)

9. (false rib)

When I was a teenager, my parents tried to take me to a hot new rib
joint in Chicago named Bones, but the line to get in was long and
we were too hungry to wait two hours for platters of sticky-spicy-
sweet baby backs. My sister, nine at the time, was visiting relatives
out of state; she called in the middle of the night, homesick, and my
mom answered the phone in her sleep. "Bones," she moaned
to my freaked-out sister—likely dreaming of the ribs
she hadn't been able to gnaw that evening.
"Booooooones!"

10. (false rib)

In Babylonian mythology, heaven and earth are crafted from
the ribs of Tiamat, the goddess of salt water and chaos.
Are we her vital organs, then? Her alveoli? Her
breath? Does her cage
ever ache with the
swell of us all?

11. (floating rib)

Maybe my tight, inflamed ribs are my body's way of trying to
protect me after I've shed the virus, each bone
a curved arm, a mother
holding me close.

12. (floating rib)

Halfway through the cremation process, the crematory operator
hooks the rib cage with a rake and stirs the body around so the
flames will lick it clean. I sweep my fingers over my own ribs
now, dig my thumbs into the aching, living tissue
between them, the place the rake will someday catch.

os sacrum

M Y BONES ARE THINNING.
Sometimes I swear I can feel them thinning, a dizzying lightness inside my body, my bones turning honeycomb, turning cobweb, turning hollow like a bird's. The technical name for this, the diagnosis I've been given, is osteopenia. Osteo for bone, penia for poverty.

Poor bones.

The word "poor" fills my great-grandmother Dora's files from the Jewish Consumptives' Relief Society, files I found after the pandemic sent me into a flurry of genealogical research, research fed by my desire to feel connected with something beyond our quarantine bubble, my desire to connect with my roots. I hadn't known Dora's name before I found it on a 1900 census. Letters from my grandmother, from her sister, from their aunt, repeatedly begged the sanatorium to keep their "poor sick mother," their "poor sick sister" there as a patient, even though they couldn't send more money for her care. They couldn't afford a train ticket to bring Dora to Chicago, either, didn't have space for Dora in their already packed home. When she died, they received a telegram saying the sanatorium could ship her body to Chicago for $138, or bury her near Denver for thirty-five dollars. They chose the latter, sending instructions to bury their "poor dead mother" with enough extra money for a stone, the same stone I'd find online 104 years later, plot C-018 of the Golden Hill Cemetery in Lakewood, Colorado.

I wasn't sure the stone was really hers—Dora Meyers was a fairly common name at the time, and as far as I knew, she had lived in Nebraska, not Colorado—but then my husband decided to join me in research, and, once again, we became a mystery-solving couple, Hart to Hart, heart to heart. He told me the cemetery held patients from the Jewish Consumptives' Relief Society's sanatorium nearby, and my poor bones knew it was her. Prior to this frenzy of research, all I had known of my great grandmother was that she had been sent to a tuberculosis sanatorium, that my grandmother and her sister were raised by an aunt and uncle in Omaha, that their brothers had been sent to an orphanage, but I had imagined the sanatorium was in Nebraska, had imagined her children could visit. (I later discovered the boys had been sent to the Jewish Orphan Asylum in Cleveland, and my grandmother had moved to Chicago with her aunt and uncle long before her mother's death. After Dora was sent to the clean air of Colorado, her children never saw her again.) The fact that this was indeed Dora's gravestone was confirmed when I found the sanatorium archives, found the letters from my grandmother and her sister in Dora's files.

The Golden in the name of the cemetery still jars me; my mother, Dora's granddaughter, took her own life in a building named Golden Oaks, and I feel a golden thread of pain strung between them. A letter from the superintendent of the sanatorium reads: "Dora Meyers died today at 2:20 a.m. She suffered severely during the last seventy-two hours. She left no statement aside from a desire for a minyan, for which purpose she left ten dollars." My mother left no statement, either. Just her severe suffering. A thousand dollars in her pocket. The desire to be gone.

I wonder who made up the minyan, the ten people who recited the Kaddish for Dora, wonder if they were patients or staff of the sanatorium, wonder if they had known Dora at all, if any of them shed tears over her grave, or if it was just a job for them, less than a dollar per person. The minyan cost $6.75; the $3.25 left over was donated to the JCRS. I wonder who carved the stone her bones rest beneath, the Hebrew letters I'm just starting to be able to decipher (learning Hebrew, learning Yiddish, being part of my pandemic genealogical quest), the flowers that look like earthy Jewish stars.

Our bones are made of stars. Half the calcium in the universe comes from calcium-rich supernovas, star ash packing our skeleton, our teeth. We are stars resurrected, the same way sea lions and yellowtail amberjack are my mother resurrected, absorbing her ashes in the water they call home.

The sanatorium kept Dora long beyond her and her family's ability to pay, citing her "acute sacroiliac disease," possibly from the tuberculosis, which can lodge not just in lungs but in bones. My own presumed COVID seems, over time, to have migrated from my lungs to my joints, triggering inflammatory arthritis, as well as costochondritis. My rheumatologist tested for tuberculosis when he ordered my blood work; the result came back "inconclusive," and I wonder if whispers of Dora's consumption still echo inside my genes.

The sacroiliac joints are where the tailbone and hip bones meet, os sacrum for "sacred bone," os ilium for "bone of the flank or groin." The Yiddish word for sacrum is teylbeyn—perhaps Dora said, "Oy, meyn teylbeyn!" a phrase I take to saying, too, as my own sacroiliac joints twinge—but the Hebrew word is luz. Luz, not meaning light, like the Spanish luz, but a word meaning almond or almond tree, something strong and fruitful, the bone dimpled like the shell of the nut. Ancient Jews believed the sacrum, the luz, holds the nucleus for resurrection of the body. In a Midrash legend, Rabbi Joshua ben Hananiah says this is because "though you grind the luz in a hand mill, it is not pulverized; though you burn it in a fire, it is not consumed; though you put it in water, it is not dissolved; though you place it on an anvil and begin to strike it with a hammer, the anvil is split and the hammer cleft, but the luz remains intact."

Dora's luz, that sacred bone, likely remains intact in plot C-018, the beautiful iliac crest flaring from it, a holy, holey bowl beneath the ground. When I see the word "iliac" I always read it first as "lilac," and I like to think of lilacs sprouting from her sacrum, flowering fragrant inside her coffin. I know I have flowered from her skeleton, too, that I am her resurrection, carrying her in my poor, thinning bones, in the burn of my joints, threads of luz, of golden star stuff, strung between us.

going to seed

on losing and finding voice
in the age of covid

"YOUR LUNGS ARE QUIET," MY DOCTOR SAID, CON-
cern in her voice.

I shivered, her stethoscope cold on my back, my shirt lifted in the parking lot behind our small mountain town hospital, skin exposed to the brisk April air. Her words hit home; it wasn't just my lungs—my whole inner world had gone quiet of late.

I had been sick for more than a month, diagnosed with presumed COVID-19 over the phone by this doctor, and over video by a TeleMed doctor on a weekend when I had taken a turn for the worse, but this was the first time a triage nurse had finally cleared me to be seen at the drive-up respiratory clinic. I was happy to find my own doctor there (once she told me it was her beneath the face shield and mask and hair covering, and I was able to recognize her familiar eyes). My absence of breath sounds was a sign of pneumonia, she said; she prescribed antibiotics for that and a painful ear infection, sending me on my way with kindness.

The antibiotics helped my ear, but there were still quite a few nights when I feared I would die in my sleep, nights when I'd wake at 3 a.m. gasping for breath, nights when I couldn't fall asleep at all because lying down exacerbated my breathing difficulties. I felt an urgency to write letters to my family to let them know how much

I love and appreciate them, little gifts for them to open after my death, but I found I couldn't translate my heart onto the page. I found I couldn't write at all.

Several years ago, I taught a seminar called "One Year to Live," in which I'd encouraged writers to use awareness of our mortality as fuel to write our most meaningful and necessary work. We don't know how much time we have on this earth, I reminded them; let's make the most of each moment. I was sure I would write like the wind if I knew I was nearing the end of my life, sure I would write like fire, write, as they say in *Hamilton*, like I was running out of time. I could picture myself in a frenzy to get all the books knocking around inside me out onto the page, writing and writing until my final breath.

This spring, when I truly thought I was dying, the words wouldn't come. I was in a daze—from the brain fog of the illness, from the lack of good sleep, from the new pandemic reality my nervous system was struggling to comprehend. Not only could I not write, but I couldn't read, either, at least not in the deep, sustained way I've read for as long as I can remember. I could read out loud to my son at bedtime, my mind barely comprehending the words that came out of my mouth, I could read and painstakingly respond to student- and freelance editing client's work, the text enlarged on my laptop to help it pierce my thick skull, but the books I wanted to read for my own pleasure or knowledge felt impenetrable. The physical page of text would become a jumble, a blur.

I felt the most alive, the most awake, when I walked my little dog, Pepper, in the narrow stretch of woods by our house. Pepper seemed to understand I needed to walk slowly, and she took her time sniffing around fallen logs and pine cone scraps left by feasting squirrels so I could catch my breath. I sniffed around in my own way, using my eyes, since I could barely smell, and I started to notice things. I noticed that what I had thought were ruffly, multilobed blossoms on the Sierra currant bushes were actual clusters of tiny, individual flowers. I noticed the stunning complexity of grasses I had long considered "boring," amazed at how their tassels were woven like intricate basketwork. I noticed that if you looked at anything closely enough, it was never boring.

My camera helped me look more intimately, zooming in to see the velvety little hairs at the base of the mountain dandelion, the bits of pink in what had seemed like a dull, white buckwheat flower, the elaborate, plumed antennae of a common brown moth. I had joked that in quarantine, I felt as if I were living in a humanely run zoo, my world confined to the indoor habitat of my house and the outdoor habitat of this little stretch of woods. But when I took the time to discover something new about this habitat every day, I didn't feel caged at all.

I often tell my students the most important part of being a writer is keeping our hearts open, our minds open, our senses open (while maintaining the healthy boundaries that support our hearts, minds, and senses) so we can stay open to inspiration, which can strike from unexpected places. I may not have been able to find many words, but my eyes were hungry to take in the world, to find images that begged to be captured. Some of these images offered a clear look at the wonder of things as they were, the plush, red alien egg of a snow plant, the intense blue of a Steller's jay's feather, while others were more metaphorical—trees that looked like dinosaurs; monster mouths inside a pine cone. I also found lessons around me—the way the gentle touch of a reed in the water left deep ripples in the creek, the way butterflies and other pollinators reminded me to combine beauty and purposefulness in my own art. Sometimes I felt moved to bring myself into a picture, my hand or arm or part of my face not central to the shot, just part of the landscape. And some words bubbled up along with this picture taking, captions for the photos that were sometimes silly and punny, that helped share my own way of seeing, my own "weirdidity," to use a word my dad coined to describe one's inherent weirdness.

Toward the end of his life, my dad told me he wished he had become a photographer because he saw things differently from other people, and he wished he had recorded that; I wish he had recorded that, too—what a gift it would have been to see the world through his eyes. I sometimes feel as if I'm channeling him as I walk these woods, phone camera at the ready, as if I'm living out this dream for him in my own simple, untrained way. But, of course, the experience is mostly for me—it's been keeping me grounded, keeping me going, through my illness and its long recovery.

I'm still dealing with lingering symptoms, still don't feel as if I've returned to my full physical or intellectual capacities. I'm not sure I ever will. I'm grateful I have this camera, grateful I have these woods, woods once walked by the Wašišiw people, people I think of often as I step where they have stepped. Even as I say, "I have these woods," I know these woods aren't mine; in fact, they're owned by the federal government, the very body that stole this land from its rightful caretakers. I want to stay aware of this, want to use my phone's camera to bear witness to and honor this land and all it holds, including its painful history.

When I had been posting these photos for a while, some friends sweetly suggested I may have a book on my hands, but I found myself resisting that idea. I wanted this new process to be what it was—a meditation, a lifeline. I thought about my mom, who came to painting late in life, who, after an intense forty days of inspired art making, thought her self-taught work belonged in the Museum of Contemporary Art. She wanted to be the new Grandma Moses. She wasn't able to allow that transformative, creative whirlwind—a stretch of time during which she felt guided by dead relatives—to be enough in itself; she wanted a more external glory. I didn't want to be like that, didn't want to expect anything more than what the process was already giving me. When my inner world hushed, that silence swept any last shred of ambition from my body. I realized that I would be okay, that I would still be me, still be whole, even if I never write or publish another book in my lifetime, something I never could have imagined myself thinking before 2020. It was—it's still—a relief to feel creative without caring about the process becoming a product, without worrying about bad reviews, or disappointing sales, or the introvert's exhaustion of public events (as much as I do love connecting with readers and the literary community). It was—it's still—a relief to just play, to know I still can play even when I'm feeling crummy and quiet inside.

I don't know if I was truly close to death this spring, but it sure felt that way. It felt that way so much, in fact, that some deep part of me seems to think I did die, as if I'm living some bizarro world, second coming of my own life now, or perhaps I'm a ghost still hanging around. I happened upon a photo of Lake Michigan recently on social media and thought, "That's where my ashes are scattered," as if I'd already been burned down to dust, been tossed into the beloved waters of my childhood. It took me a couple of moments to realize what a weird thought that had been, to realize that no, that hasn't happened, not yet. I've been noticing lots of scatterings in the woods of late, salsify and prairie goldenrod going to seed, their colorful blossoms turned to pale puffballs, those puffballs taking to the wind. I've been thinking about how the phrase "going to seed" has been used in such a negative way, akin to "letting oneself go"—why is it so bad to go to seed, when that's such an act of generosity and hope, sending the stuff of life out so future generations can flourish? Why is it so bad to let one's self go? Don't we sometimes hold on to our selves too tightly, not allowing them to change or grow or evolve or show the impact of time? This stretch of pandemic time has affected me greatly—I can see it in my hair, in my skin, in the tiredness of my eyes. I can feel it in the way words are still tricky to put together, in the way I'm reaching toward image instead. I'm letting my self go and seeing what's left behind. I've snapped a few photos of flowers after all of their seeds had taken to the air, and their centers are still there, the integrity of their structures still strong. I've come to appreciate the spare, elegant beauty of what remains after a flower's expected beauty has fallen away, after it's given all it can to the world.

I don't think I'm there quite yet. I know—at least, I hope!—I still have some life kicking around in me, that I still have some time, still have much to give, even from an inner landscape that still feels hushed. I trust the words will continue to trickle and maybe someday flow again, trust I'll continue to find joy and discovery and inspiration in keeping my senses and mind and heart open for as long as I can muster. I no longer imagine I'd write in a frenzy if I learned I had a year (or less) to live, though. That thought no longer even appeals to me. The world doesn't *need* more of my voice, more of my books, but perhaps it does need me to empower other voices, to create space for voices that have been too often marginalized, to amplify voices that call for justice. As much as writing has meant to me my whole life, as much as it's helped me bear witness and make sense of the world within and around me (and as much as I trust it will continue to do so), I wouldn't want to spend the bulk of my dwindling days looking down at a piece of paper or ahead at a screen; I'd want to spend more time being in the world, being with the people I love. I'd want them to know how much I love them even if I'm never able to write those letters for them to open after I'm gone.

I recently took a photo of a salsify plant that had flowers in two different stages of being, one of which had already released all its seeds, its center stripped bare; the other still in a tight, green bud, yet to open. I resonated with that salsify, one foot firmly in this world, one on its way out, one part of me spent, another part eager for what's to come. My walks in the woods remind me about cycles, how lupines burst into brilliant color, then fade; how birds build nests, and nestlings hatch and fly off to build their own nests;

how bare branches turn to leaf turn to blossom turn to berry; how berry disappears into the mouth of bird or bear; how they drop the seeds elsewhere, how those seeds take root. How we're part of all of it—all this budding, all this flowering; all this generous falling away.

works cited

Epigraph

HÉLÈNE CIXOUS: "COMING TO WRITING" AND OTHER ESSAYS, edited by Deborah Jenson, with an Introductory Essay by Susan Rubin Suleiman, translated by Sarah Cornell, Deborah Jenson, Ann Liddle, and Susan Sellers, Cambridge, Mass.: Harvard University Press, Copyright © 1991 by the President and Fellows of Harvard College. Used by permission. All rights reserved.

"Drawing Breath"

Rumi, Jelaluddin Balkhi. *The Essential Rumi.* Trans. Coleman Barks. New York: Quality Paperback Book Club, 1998. Used with permission.

Rukeyser, Muriel. "Poem Out of Childhood." *Out of Silence: Selected Poems.* Evanston, IL: Triquarterly Books/Northwestern University, 1992. Used by permission of William L. Rukeyser.

Ackerman, Diane. *A Natural History of the Senses.* New York: Vintage, 1990. Used with permission.

Abram, David. *The Spell of the Sensuous: Perception and Language in a More-Than-Human World.* NY: Pantheon, 1996. Used with permission.

Parthan, Baiju. "Living in Sacred Time." *Humanscape Magazine.* March 1999 <http://www.humanscapeindia.org/hs1299/hs12992t.htm>.

Steinman, Louise. *The Knowing Body.* Boston: Shambhala, 1986. Used with permission.

Carson, Anne. *Eros the Bittersweet.* Normal, IL: Dalkey Archive, 1998. Used with permission of the Dalkey Archive.

Rilke, Rainer Maria. *Sonnets to Orpheus.* Trans. M.D., Herter Norton. New York: Norton, 1942. Used with permission.

Hirshfield, Jane. *Nine Gates: Entering the Mind of Poetry.* New York: HarperCollins, 1997. Used with permission.

Ehrlich, Gretel. "Life at Close Range." *The Writer on Her Work, Volume II: New Essays in New Territory.* Ed. Janet Sternburg. New York: Norton, 1991. 175-179. Excerpt from "Life at Close Range" by Gretel

Ehrlich from *The Writer on Her Work Volume II: New Essays in New Territory* (ed. Janet Sternburg.) Copyright © 1992 by Gretel Ehrlich. Originally published by W.W. Norton & Company, 1992. Used courtesy of Darhansoff & Verrill Literary Agents. All rights reserved.

Ginsberg, Allen. Interview. *Book Show*. NPR, New York. 24 January 1994.

Hirsch, Edward. *How to Read a Poem: And Fall in Love with Poetry*. New York: Harcourt Brace, 1999. Used with permission.

Jonson, Ben. *The English Grammar. London, [s.n], 1640.*

Ginsberg, Allen. Interview. *Writers at Work: The Paris Review Interviews*. Ed. Kay Dick. Middlesex, England: Penguin Books, 1972.

Birkerts, Sven. *The Gutenberg Elegies.* New York: Fawcett Columbine, 1994. Used by permission of the author.

Iyer, Pico. "In Praise of the Humble Comma." *The Eloquent Essay*. Ed. John Loughery. New York: Persea Books, 2000. Used with permission.

D'Ambrosio, Charles. "Interview with Charlie D'Ambrosio." Excerpt 11 July 2000. <http://www.english.swt.edu/excerpt.dir/dambros1.htm>.

HÉLÈNE CIXOUS: "COMING TO WRITING" AND OTHER ESSAYS, edited by Deborah Jenson, with an Introductory Essay by Susan Rubin Suleiman, translated by Sarah Cornell, Deborah Jenson, Ann Liddle, and Susan Sellers, Cambridge, Mass.: Harvard University Press, Copyright © 1991 by the President and Fellows of Harvard College. Used by permission. All rights reserved.

Lowen, Alexander, M.D. *The Betrayal of the Body*. New York: Macmillan, 1967. Permission is granted by the Alexander Lowen Foundation.

Hong, Peggy Gwi-Seok. "Why I Dance." Unpublished poem. Used by permission of Peggy Gwi-Seok Hong.

Harjo, Joy. "Fire." *Sisters of the Earth*. Ed. Lorraine Anderson. New York: Vintage, 1991. "Fire" from WHAT MOON DROVE ME TO THIS? by Joy Harjo-Sapulpa. Copyright © 1979 Joy Harjo-Sapulpa, used by permission of The Wylie Agency LLC.

Allen, Paul Gunn. *The Sacred Hoop: Recovering the Feminine in American Indian Traditions*. Beacon Press, 1992. Reprinted by permission of Beacon Press, Boston.

Moyers, Bill. *The Language of Life: A Festival of Poets*. New York: Doubleday, 1995. Used with permission.

Shacochis, Bob. "Breathing Space." *The Writing Life*. Ed. Neil Baldwin and Diane Osen. New York: Random House, 1995. Used by permission of the author.

"Thunder, Thighs"

Pfahler, Ruth. *Special Diet for Thighs and Hips*. Self-published. 1953.

The Griffith Ramayana. Trans. Ralph TH Griffith. London: EJ Lazarus & Co, 1870.

Budge, Sir Ernest. *The Gods of the Egyptians, Or, Studies in Egyptian Mythology*. London: Methuen & Co, 1904.

"Body Dysmorphic Disorder." Anxiety & Depression Association of America. <https://adaa.org/understanding-anxiety/body-dysmorphic-disorder>. Used with permission.

Graham, Michelle. *Wanting to Be Her*. Westmont, IL: IVP Books, 2005. Used with permission.

Wells, Veronica. "Do Black Girls Want a Thigh Gap?" *MadameNoire*. 26 Feb 2014. <https://madamenoire.com/405008/do-black-girls-want-a-thigh-gap/>

"We Too"

Miller, Laura. "The Last Word: We the Characters." *The New York Times*. 18 April 2004. <https://www.nytimes.com/2004/04/18/books/the-last-word-we-the-characters.html>.

Subramanian, Mathangi. *A People's History of Heaven*. Chapel Hill, NC: Algonquin Books, 2019. Reprinted by permission of Algonquin Books, an imprint of Hachette Book Group, Inc.

Shea, Renee H. "The Urgency of Knowing: A Profile of Julie Otsuka." *Poets & Writers*. Sept/Oct 2011. <https://www.pw.org/content/urgency_of_knowing_a_profile_of_julie_otsuka>.

Atwood, Margaret. "Romantic Idealism, Barnyard Realism." *The New York Times*. 12 June 1983. <https://archive.nytimes.com/www.nytimes.com/books/98/12/06/specials/chase-queen.html>.

Mirvis, Tova. *The Ladies Auxiliary*. New York: W.W. Norton & Co, 1999. Used with permission.

Díaz, Jaquira. *Ordinary Girls*. Chapel Hill, NC: Algonquin Books, 2019. Reprinted by permission of Algonquin Books, an imprint of Hachette Book Group, Inc.

Bennett, Brit. *The Mothers*. New York: Riverhead, 2016. Used with permission.

Atwood, Margaret. *The Penelopiad*. London: Faber & Faber, 2007. Used with permission.

Brown, Eleanor. *The Weird Sisters*. London: Penguin Adult, 2011. Used with permission.

Nesbit, Tara Shea. *The Wives of Los Alamos*. London: Bloomsbury, 2014. Used with permission of Bloomsbury Publishing, Inc.

Atkinson, Kate. "Amazon Exclusive: Kate Atkinson Interviews Laura Lippman." Amazon, 2011. <https://www.amazon.com/dp/B0070R0240/ref=dp-kindle-redirect?_encoding=UTF8&btkr=1>

Barrett, Andrea. *The Air We Breathe*. New York: W.W. Norton & Co, 2007. Used with permission.

Otsuka, Julie. *The Buddha in the Attic*. New York: Knopf, 2011. Used with permission.

Solnit, Rebecca. *Whose Story is This? Old Conflicts, New Chapters*. Chicago: Haymarket Books, 2019. Used with permission.

"Her Shadow"

Danticat, Edwidge. *The Art of Death*. Minneapolis: Graywolf Press, 2017. Used with permission.

Lyden, Jacki. *Daughter of the Queen of Sheba*. Boston: Houghton Mifflin, 1997. Used with permission.

Tan, Amy. *The Opposite of Fate*. London: Penguin Books, 2004. Copyright © 1993 by Amy Tan. First appeared in Ski Magazine. Reprinted by permission of the author and the Sandra Dijkstra Literary Agency.

Slater, Lauren. *Lying*. New York: Random House, 2000. Used with permission.

Spiegelman, Nadja. *I'm Supposed to Protect You From All of This*. New York: Riverhead, 2016. Used with permission.

Solnit, Rebecca. *The Faraway Nearby*. New York: Viking, 2013. Used with permission.

Williams, Terry Tempest. *Refuge*. New York: Pantheon, 2000. Used with permission.

Jarrell, Andrea. *I'm the One Who Got Away*. Berkeley: She Writes Press, 2017. Used with permission.

Sexton, Linda Gray. *Searching for Mercy Street*. Boston: Little, Brown, & Co, 1994. From "Searching for Mercy Street: My Journey Back to My Mother, Anne Sexton", copyright © 1994, 2011 by Linda Gray Sexton. Published by Counterpoint. Used by permission of the author. All rights reserved.

Gore, Ariel. *The End of Eve*. Portland: Hawthorne Books, 2014. Used with permission.

Smith, Tracy K. *Ordinary Light*. New York, Knopf, 2015. Used with permission.

Kincaid, Jamaica. *Annie John*. New York: FS&G, 1997. Used with permission.

"Get Me Away From Here, I'm Dying"

Belle and Sebastian. Writers: David Stuart, Cooke Michael John, Colburn Richard William, Geddes Christopher Thomas, Jackson Stephen Thomas, Martin Sarah Ann, Murdoch Stuart Lee, and Campbell Isobel Karen. "Get Me Away from Here, I'm Dying." *If You're Feeling Sinister*. Matador Records, 1996.

"Joy"

Staggs, Sam. *Inventing Elise Maxwell*. New York: Macmillan, 2012. Used with permission.

Turin, Luca and Tania Sanchez. *Perfume: An A-Z Guide*. New York: Viking, 2008. Used with permission.

Demachy, François. Press release. Dior. 2018.

Behnke, Mark. "New Perfume Review: Joy by Dior—Shaking My Head." *Colognoisseur*. 27 Aug 2018. <https://colognoisseur.com/new-perfume-review-joy-by-dior-shaking-my-head/>.

"Joy Jean Patou." Fragrantica. <https://www.fragrantica.com/perfume/Jean-Patou/Joy-1436.html>

"Anniversary Gifts"

Field, Ann and Gretchen Scoble. *The Meaning of Wedding Anniversaries*. San Francisco: Chronicle, 2003. Used with permission from Chronicle Books, LLC.

"All That She Wants"

Ace of Base. "All That She Wants." *Happy Nation*. Mega Records, 1992.

Kraus, Chris. *I Love Dick*. Los Angeles: Semiotext(e), 1997. Used with permission.

Cixous, Hélène. "Laugh of the Medusa." *Signs*. Trans. Keith Cohen and Paula Cohen. Chicago: University of Chicago Press, 1976. Used with permission.

Ferguson, Luna M. *Me, Myself, They: Life Beyond the Binary*. Toronto: House of Anansi Press, 2019. Excerpt from page 106 of Me, Myself, They copyright © 2019 by Luna Ferguson. Reproduced with permission from House of Anansi Press, Toronto. www.houseofanansi.com

Murphy, Bernadette. *Harley & Me*. Los Angeles: Counterpoint, 2016. Used with permission.

Frangello, Gina. *Blow Your House Down*. Los Angeles: Counterpoint, 2021. Used with permission.

Dederer, Claire. *Love and Trouble*. New York: Knopf, 2017. Used with permission.

Loh, Sandra Tsing. *The Madwoman in the Volvo*. New York: W.W. Norton & Co, 2014. Used with permission.

Scanlon, Suzanne. *Her Thirty-Seventh Year*. Blacksburg, Virginia: Noemi Press, 2015. Used with permission.

Matthewson, Melissa. *Tracing the Desire Line*. Ralston, Omaha: Split Lip Press, 2019. Used with permission.

Lorde, Audre. "Uses of the Erotic." *Sister Outsider*. Trumansburg, New York: The Crossing Press, 1984. Used with permission.

"My Parents' Delusions"

Manguso, Sarah. *Ongoingness*. Minneapolis: Graywolf Press, 2015. Used with permission.

"Rib/Cage"

Diaz, Natalie. "Postcolonial Love Poem." *Postcolonial Love Poem*. Minneapolis: Graywolf Press, 2020. Used with permission.

about the author

gayle brandeis is the author most recently of the memoir *The Art of Misdiagnosis* (Beacon Press), and the novel in poems *Many Restless Concerns* (Black Lawrence Press), shortlisted for the Shirley Jackson Award. Earlier books include the poetry collection *The Selfless Bliss of the Body* (Finishing Line Press), the writer's craft book *Fruitflesh: Seeds of Inspiration for Women Who Write* (HarperOne) and the novels *The Book of Dead Birds* (HarperCollins), which won the PEN/Bellwether Prize judged by Barbara Kingsolver, Toni Morrison, and Maxine Hong Kingston, *Self Storage* (Ballantine), *Delta Girls* (Ballantine), and *My Life with the Lincolns* (Henry Holt BYR), chosen as a state-wide read in Wisconsin. Gayle's essays, poetry, and short fiction have been widely published in places such as *The Guardian, The New York Times, The Washington Post, O (The Oprah Magazine), The Rumpus, Salon,* and more. She has received numerous honors, including the Columbia Journal Nonfiction Award, a Barbara Mandigo Kelly Peace Poetry Award, Notable Essays in Best American Essays 2016, 2019, and 2020, the QPB/ Story Magazine Short Story Award and the 2018 Multi Genre Maverick Writer Award. She was named A Writer Who Makes a Difference by The Writer Magazine, and served as Inlandia Literary Laureate from 2012-2014, focusing on bringing writing workshops to underserved communities. She lives in Highland Park, IL teaches in the low residency MFA programs at Antioch University and University of Nevada, Reno at Lake Tahoe.

acknowledgments

The word "conspire" literally means "to breathe together." So many people conspired with me to make this book possible, breathing life into its pages and into me (both in person and from afar). I'm so happy to be able to thank them here.

Thank you to everyone at Overcup Press for all of your generous support—to Pat McDonald and Rachel Bell for inviting me into the Overcup family with such open arms, to Des Hewson for being such an insightful and supportive editor, to the rest of the team for supporting me and this collection. I'm so grateful to have found such a loving home for this project of my heart. Deep thanks, too, to Liz Prato, whose Twitter takeover let me know Overcup was looking for books like this one, and to my magical agent, Laurie Fox, who tied everything together with a beautiful bow and a gorgeous sprinkling of pixie dust. Thank you, too, to Cassie Mannes Murray for helping me get the word out with such enthusiasm.

I wish I could thank each and every person in my writing community; I'm so lucky and grateful to have so many talented, beloved friends and students in my life. I want to shine a special spotlight of gratitude on a few folks who helped with essays in this collection and/or provided emotional support during the times that led me to write these essays over the last twenty years: Laraine Herring, June Saraceno, Suzanne Roberts, Alma Luz Villanueva, Jane O'Shields-Hayner, Grace Saahira Tedder, Catherine Kineavy, Cati Porter, Anjali Alban, Lidia Yuknavitch, Jen Pastiloff, Jane Ratcliffe, Amy Shimshon-Santo, Bernadette Murphy, Peggy Gwi-Seok Hong, Leta Seletzky, Kate Maruyama, Karrie Higgins,

GAYLE BRANDEIS

Peter Selgin, Brian Turner. Making lists like this always feels good but terrifying—I'm so worried I've forgotten to mention dear, important people in my life; if I have, please accept my deepest apologies and deepest gratitude and know you shine in my heart. Thank you to all my students and colleagues, past and present, at Antioch University, Sierra Nevada University, University of Nevada, Reno, PEN Malawi, LitReactor, Fine Arts Work Center, University of California, Riverside/Palm Desert, the University of Redlands, UCLA Extension Writers' Program (and everywhere else I've ever taught over the many years of writing these essays) for being awesome and inspiring. Thank you to all my friends on social media; your friendship feels real, not virtual, and I'm so grateful for it. Thank you to my different writing groups and all my mentors over the years—your light still guides me. Thank you to my former agents, who were each such passionate champions of my work. Thank you to all the women at the Saint Mary's writing retreats—I love having written with you in that haunted place.

Additional thanks to Laraine Herring for her class, "Breath, Blood, Bones & Bodies: A Multi-Genre Generative into our Ghost-Genes" via Literary Kitchen, during which I wrote "Sugar in the Blood" and "Os Sacrum," and to Chelsea T. Hicks for her class "Writing With Our Ancestors" via Corporeal Writing, during which I wrote the parenthetical parts of "Sugar in the Blood." Both classes came at the perfect time.

Deep thanks to the editors who published essays from this collection, and offered suggestions that made my work better (in alphabetical order by journal): Dinty Moore and Julie Riddle at *Brevity;* Jinwoo Chong and Shir Mina Orner at *Columbia Journal* (with special thanks to Emily Maloney for choosing my essay for the *Columbia Journal* 2021 Spring Nonfiction Prize); David Griffith and Ander Monson at *Essay Daily/DIAGRAM;* Jennifer Niesslein at *Full Grown People;* Roxane Gay and Laura June Topolsky at *Gay Mag;* Chad Sweeney at *Ghost Town* literary

222

magazine; Joy Manne at *The Healing Breath*; Frederick Spears at *Jam Tarts*; Taylor Pavlik and Rebecca Rubenstein at *Midnight Breakfast*; Chelsey Clammer, Seth Fischer, and Erika Kleinman at *The Nervous Breakdown*; Stephanie Gibson and Kathleen Kuo at Nevada Humanities *Heart to Heart*; Daniel Jones, Miya Lee, and Roberta Zeff at *The New York Times*; Sophie Beck and Steven Church at *The Normal School*; Cynthia Bargar at *Pangyrus*; Arielle Bernstein and Julie Greicius at *The Rumpus*; Kate Moses and Camille Peri at *Salon*; Allison Klein at *The Washington Post* (and Nicholas DiSabatino at Beacon Press for connecting us); Michelle Tudor at *Wildness*. Deep thanks, too, to all who read and shared these essays when they were originally published, and to the readers who reached out to me personally to share their own stories in return—that is always such a gift.

I can't even begin to express how grateful I am for my beloved family, the people with whom I can breathe most freely—my whole, wonderful mishpucha of cousins/nieces/nephews/niblings/in-laws; my amazing siblings Elizabeth, Jon, and Sue, and their amazing partners Craig, Magdalene, and the late Larry; my wondrous kids, Asher, Hannah, Arin (and his wondrous wife, Prany!); my sweet, foxy, patient, phenomenal husband, Michael, who regularly takes my breath away. How lucky I am to love and be loved by you all.